MINIATURE SCHNAUZER

FROM THE EDITORS OF FANCY MAGAZINE

CONTENTS

Miniature Schnauzer, a Smart Owner's Guide™
part of the Kennel Club Books® Interactive Series™
ISBN: 978-1-593787-74-5. ©2010

Kennel Club Books, 40 Broad St., Freehold, NJ 07728. Printed in China.

*photographers include Isabelle Francias/BowTie Inc.; Tara Darling/BowTie Inc.;
Gina Cioli and Pamela Hunnicutt/BowTie Inc. Contributing writer: Muriel P. Lee*

For CIP information, see page 176.

K9 EXPERT

Woo-woo, woo-woo! In Miniature Schnauzer talk that means "so happy you like me and want me to join your family." And if you're considering getting one of these cuties, it's best to think of it just that way.

The Miniature Schnauzer wants to be part of the family and will do his best to add a new loving element to yours.

Although most Miniature Schnauzers look quite similar – whether solid black, salt and pepper, or black and silver – their temperaments can vary dramatically. If you have an energetic, very terrier-like dog, that's perfectly normal. But if your little schnauzer is just the sweetest, calmest thing ever, he's absolutely OK, too. That's one of the charms of this breed.

Because Minis didn't "go to ground," meaning tunnel into rodents' holes, they're not typically diggers. That's good news for any dog owner. And because their terrier ties aren't as strong as other breeds in this feisty group, Minis often tend toward herding and other working dog behaviors. These traits can make them great family dogs.

Many Mini owners swear that this breed is actually a little old man wearing a dog costume!

EDUCATION

Regardless of temperament, your new pal wants to make you happy. With positive training, he'll learn to follow your household's rules and be a wonderful companion for many years to come.

Even with all that excellent training, be certain you always, always, always keep your Mini on a leash or in a securely fenced area. He will be so in tune with the world around him, curious about every scent and sound, that given the chance, he'll dash off to check them out. To guarantee his safety, keep him restrained – at all times.

He'll be a happier pet, though, if he can get some exercise in safe off-leash venues. Want to try a dog sport? You've got the right breed. Agility, competitive obedience and flyball can be fun, as well as provide good exercise for your Miniature Schnauzer. Just remember that all of these activities must be within an enclosure or building. That way, he can safely enjoy any activity you want to do with him. For the super-active Minis, sports put all that energy to good use.

You'll need to decide if you want to keep your dog's fabulous wiry coat – learning to strip it yourself or paying a groomer to do it – or let it go a little softer with more typical care. Similarly, the classic trim of his beard, mustache and bushy eyebrows can be maintained by a professional or by you – if you're up to it. Either way, don't let his coat fool you, this breed takes a lot of grooming.

But fear not. When you walk your dapper little fellow down the street to the admiring glances, and *oohs* and *aahs* of passersby, all your training and coat care will be worthwhile. And your new canine friend will be very proud and happy that you invited him

With this Smart Owner's Guide™, you are well on your way to getting your Mini Schnauzer diploma.
But your schnauzer education doesn't end here.

You're invited to join in **Club Schnauzer**™ (DogChannel.com/Club-Schnauzer), a FREE online site with lots of fun and instructive features such as:
◆ **forums, blogs** and **profiles** where you can connect with other Miniature Schnauzer owners
◆ **downloadable charts** and **checklists** to help you be a smart and loving Miniature Schnauzer owner
◆ access to Miniature Schnauzer **e-cards** and **wallpapers**
◆ interactive **games**
◆ canine **quizzes**

The **Smart Owner's Guide** series and **Club Schnauzer** are backed by the experts at DOG FANCY® magazine and DogChannel.com — who have been providing trusted and up-to-date information about dogs and dog people for more than 40 years. Log on and join the club today!

to become a member of your family. Enjoy every moment of your new adventure!

Susan Chaney
Editor, DOG FANCY

CHAPTER 1

MINI SIDES TO

A SCHNAUZER

It's a fact that most Miniature Schnauzers have outsized personalities, but that doesn't mean that those personalities are identical. In fact, according to Rich Edwards, who is the vice president of the Mount Vernon Miniature Schnauzer Club, the case is quite the opposite. Edwards, who lives in Laytonsville, Md., says that of the eight Miniature Schnauzers he's lived with, each had or has a different personality.

"Zachary, our first, was the happiest dog we'd ever met," he says. "He considered everyone, young and old, his friend. Dallas wants little attention and can be an independent and stubborn little cuss. He once lifted his leg on his handler in the show ring during competition. Travis, on the other hand, will go happily into the show ring with anyone willing to hold his lead, and at home, he will sit in your lap for hours.

"And Roubi is a sweet, loving dog without the licking. When Roubi was shown she would at times announce her presence in the ring with a single bark. And she has been known to put her front paws on a judge's leg and look up at the person as if to say 'thank you for the ribbon!'"

it's a Fact

Most Mini pups are born black. Salt and peppers will usually have some tan or fawn shadings with light spots over the eyes. Black and silvers also have these facial spots but solid blacks exhibit no such color variations.

Despite such personality differences, however, Miniature Schnauzers do have some traits in common.

● **This bred loves attention.** Edwards's Dallas notwithstanding, most breeders agree that Miniature Schnauzers lap up any and all attention from their people. "They will go out of their way to get it," says Mini owner Judy Sousa from Saratoga, Calif. "I like placing my puppies with families that have children, because I know that with kids, the puppy is more likely to get the attention he wants."

● **They sound the alarm.** Most Miniature Schnauzers appear to believe that they have a sacred duty to tell their people about any and all possible intrusions onto their home territory — generally by barking. "They make excellent watchdogs," says Evelyn Hoover, breeder referral and rescue coordinator for the Lone Star Miniature Schnauzer Club of Dallas, Texas. "Mine lets me know when the postman is a block up the street."

● **They want to connect.** "What I love about Miniature Schnauzers is that they really, really want to please you," says Marge Moenter, former president of the Chicago Miniature Schnauzer Club. "The eye contact with a Mini Schnauzer is so special, and I've not had that with other breeds."

Did You Know?

The Mini is No. 1! The Standard Schnauzer may have come first in history. The Giant Schnauzer may come in a much larger size. But the Miniature Schnauzer, well, she rules — at least in popularity. In her short but peppy history, the Mini has enjoyed a meteoric rise, consistently hovering in or near the top 10 most popular breeds in the United States. Credit her sparkling personality, her scruffy charisma, her convenient size, her deeply rooted affection for the people in her life — whatever the reason, the Miniature Schnauzer is here to stay.

Meet other Mini owners just like you. On our Mini forums, you can chat about your Miniature Schnauzer and ask other owners for advice on training, health issues and anything else about your favorite dog breed. Log onto **DogChannel.com/Club-Schnauzer** for details!

● **They're terrier "lite."** The Miniature Schnauzer is a member of the American Kennel Club's Terrier Group, but devotees of this breed claim that they're not as terrier-like as other breeds in the group. "Most terrier people pooh-pooh calling Miniature Schnauzers terriers," Moenter says. "They say they don't have the real terrier attitude and are too laidback."

● **They love the chase.** Although Miniature Schnauzers' behavior may not fully embody that of a typical terrier, they do carry one terrier-like trait. "They're natural mousers, if given the opportunity," Moenter says. Hoover points out that some Mini Schnauzers extend their chasing talents beyond rodent harassment. "They love to chase and terrorize cats and squirrels," she says. "And they are very quick — so their victims had better be [equally] quick. Mine will stand at attention for hours if a squirrel teases him from the top of my fence."

Like so many other breeds, at least some of the Miniature Schnauzer's present-day temperament traits result directly from the breed's past. Some 200 years ago, German farmers developed these dogs to keep rats and other vermin out of their barns. Later,

Did You Know?

According to the American Kennel Club standard, three colors are acceptable: salt and pepper, black and silver, and solid black. In the salt-and-pepper coloration, the hairs are banded with black towards the tips and white towards the body with some solid black or white hairs mixed in. Although this is the breed's most common color, most people think of a solid silver or light gray when they envision this dog. This is because the majority of pet Minis are clippered when groomed, a process which not only changes the hard texture of the outer coat but removes the peppery appearance as well. The coat color lightens because the clipper removes the harsh, wiry outer coat, leaving the soft silvery gray undercoat instead. The hard topcoat of a black and silver or a solid black Mini is not banded like that of the salt-and-pepper variety; and their undercoats are a solid black.

Some rescued minis will be mixes and not have the true schnauzer colors. That doesn't mean that they won't be a great pet!

Show your artistic side. Share photos, videos and artwork of your favorite breed on Club Schnauzer. You can also submit jokes, riddles and even poetry about Miniature Schnauzers. Browse through our various galleries and see the talent of fellow Mini owners. Go to **DogChannel.com/Club-Schnauzer** and click on "Galleries" to get started.

the Mini became adept at guarding small farms and the families who lived on them, and at catching any rats that had the audacity to enter the farm house. With his small size, the Mini Schnauzer was a perfect rodent hunter. By living with people and taking on the job of guarding their families and their turf, they evolved into the people-loving, attention-seeking, alarm-conscious dogs they are today.

ONE POPULAR PUP WITH POTENTIAL PROBLEMS

While the Miniature Schnauzer attracts thousands of devotees — for the past several years, they've been the most popular terriers registered to the AKC — they do have their challenges. Chief among these less-than-desirable qualities may be their vocal prowess, which breeders agree can be a real problem. "I could do without the barking," says Beth Santure, president of the Miniature Schnauzer Club of Michigan. "I always tell people that if they want a dog that doesn't bark, they don't want a Miniature Schnauzer."

Another possible problem might be relating to children. "Most people think all Miniature Schnauzers are good with kids, but this is not always true," Hoover says. "They do not like the quick movements made by the very young, nor the screaming and yelling."

However, breeders agree that early training and socialization can do a lot to alleviate both excessive barking and a distaste for juveniles. "If puppies are raised with children, Miniature Schnauzers make great and loyal pets," Moenter says. "[And] they can be trained not to bark [so much]. You still want a warning system, and a Miniature Schnauzer will always be your announcer. However, they can be trained not to bark inappropriately from early puppyhood. I know because I have done it."

Even for those Minis who are not excessively verbal or don't have children issues, obedience training — preferably from an early age — is extremely beneficial. "Any puppy needs good training from the get-go," Moenter says. "I always recommend puppy kindergarten to my puppy buyers — the earlier, the better. Start at 12 weeks of age. Puppy kindergarten, if it is a good one, focuses on teaching the owners how to train their puppy to respond to the simple cues of come, sit, down, stay and how to walk correctly on a leash. A well-trained dog is a happy dog. I try to reinforce that with the puppy buyers."

Buying a Mini puppy from a responsible breeder is equally important. "Miniature Schnauzer breeders have been breeding not only for beauty but also for good health and for good temperament," Moenter says. "If you buy from a responsible breeder, you will find all three qualities in your puppy. And what is most important, you will have a person you can count on for any help or advice for the life of your puppy."

NOTABLE & QUOTABLE

I eat at my computer a lot and the first thing the dogs do when I let them out of their crates is to race in and see what's on the floor. If something's left out, it's fair game. I came home once and had forgotten to put away the dog [treat] training bag. It had been thoroughly gone through and every last crumb was gone. They do ferret out food. – Miniature owner and agility competitor Lynn Tamms from Oshkosh, Wisc.

No Miniature Schnauzer has won Best In Show at America's top conformation event, the Westminster Kennel Club Dog Show, but one did come in second at England's biggest show, Crufts, in 1980.

HOME, SWEET HOME

Of course, Mini Schnauzer puppies are at their best when they have the opportunity to grow up and live in homes with owners who are committed to socializing, training and caring for them. However, all homes are not created equal. Experienced breeders are clear in specifying what sorts of home they want their Mini puppies to go to — and which homes they want to avoid.

"The ideal home would be one where the owners are willing to spend time attending to their schnauzer's need for attention and love," Edwards says. "The Miniature Schnauzer owner must also be willing to train and discipline his or her dog as the dog will need reminding from time to time that [the human] is the 'alpha dog.' A commitment to grooming the Miniature Schnauzer is also important since their coats can easily become tangled and matted if not given regular attention."

Santure maintains that Mini Schnauzers fit into just about any home situation. "However," she says, "I never recommend any breed of dog if the people are not willing to put in the necessary time and effort to raise and train a dog properly."

Sousa likes her puppies to have plenty of human company. "The ideal home has someone around during the day: a retired person, someone who works from home or kids who come home from school mid-afternoon," she says.

What constitutes a less-than-ideal home? "In general, anyone not willing to make the commitment to the proper care and maintenance that the Miniature Schnauzer requires should not own one," Edwards says. "Some breeds, and the Miniature Schnauzer is one, require a higher level of commitment than others."

Santure has more specific criteria. Among those she says should not have a Miniature Schnauzer are people who want a dog that lives outdoors. "While Minis love the outdoors, they should live indoors with their family," she says. "Also, those people who will not spend the time to properly raise and train a Miniature Schnauzer. Beware: If you don't train the dog, the dog will train you."

THE MINI TRAITS OF A MINI

Every dog is an individual, and the Miniature Schnauzer is no exception. Still, most representatives of this breed share some traits that offer breed-specific challenges and joys to those who have the privilege of

The Mini has that classic beard-
ed-old-man schnauzer face!

living with them. If you're thinking of adding one of these dogs to your family, here's some of what you should expect:

● **A talented watchdog.** The Mini Schnauzer's devotion to his family and naturally alert temperament make him a natural canine sentry.

● **A motormouth.** Sometimes the Miniature Schnauzer is a little too enthusiastic about sounding the alarm or otherwise expressing his opinion. "No-bark" lessons during your Mini's puppyhood can help curb this tendency.

● **Rodent extinction.** If any mice in your home happen to encounter your Miniature Schnauzer, those mice will be toast.

● **Plenty of spunk.** Mini Schnauzers may be more laidback than some of their larger terrier cousins, but they've still got plenty of spirit. A wise owner will expect his or her dog to be inquisitive, busy and eager to be part of any and all household action.

● **Grooming bills.** Although the Miniature Schnauzer doesn't shed much, he needs more in the way of grooming than many other breeds do. In addition to regular brushing, regular appointments with a professional groomer are needed to keep him looking and feeling his best.

Leader of the Pack

Every four years, the Kansas State University College of Veterinary Medicine presents a first-year student with a renewable scholarship that honors a Miniature Schnauzer. The dog's name was Leader, and he was a 1984 gift that then-Secretary of Transportation Elizabeth Dole presented to her husband, then-Sen. Bob Dole (R-Kansas). However, Leader was not just a canine token of affection from Mrs. Dole to her husband. She presented the 2-year-old Miniature Schnauzer, whom she had adopted from a local animal shelter, to Sen. Dole when he was elected Majority Leader of the U.S. Senate.

Leader quickly became quite a dog-about-town. He would ride to work with both of the Doles as photographers snapped pictures of him sitting in the back seat of the car. The sociable, inquisitive Miniature Schnauzer — who bonded especially closely with Sen. Dole — not only became a fixture on Capitol Hill but also attended press conferences, meetings and social events all over the nation's capital. With all of this gallivanting, together with his high-profile human companions and his own jaunty personality, Leader became a media sensation. He appeared on the pages of *The Washington Post*, *USA Today*, *Newsweek* and *Time*. He even appeared as a guest on the CNN *Larry King Live* show.

Leader also attained the ultimate honor in Washington, D.C., companion animal society: He served as honorary chair of The Bark Ball, an annual fundraising event that benefits the work of the Washington Humane Society. The event draws many of the capital's most prominent human residents from the worlds of politics, media and entertainment, as well as their dogs — but unlike many such events, the atmosphere is totally bipartisan.

In fact, the human co-chairs of the 2007 event were former Clinton Administration presidential aide James Carville and his wife, longtime Republican official Mary Matalin. Other honorary chairs — all of whom are animal companions to Washington luminaries — have included Millie Bush (canine companion to former President and Mrs. George H.W. Bush); Spot Fetcher and Barney Bush (canine companions to former President and Mrs. George W. Bush); and Socks Clinton (feline companion to former President and Mrs. William J. Clinton).

Speaking of Socks, in 1996 he and Leader went paw-to-paw in a popularity contest that paralleled the presidential contest between Pres. Clinton and Sen. Dole. The senator featured his canine companion in many of his speeches, promising audiences that he would "put a Leader in the White House." During the campaign, television host John McLaughlin moderated a televised debate as to which animal made a better first pet: a cat or a dog. Viewers were able to express their preferences by telephoning their

Bob and Elizabeth Dole pose with their Mini Leader.

votes for a cost of 75 cents per call, all of which benefited WHS. According to Mary Vincent, a neighbor and friend of the Doles, Leader won that contest with 55.2 percent of the vote. (Unfortunately for Dole, he wasn't so popular, losing the presidential election with only 40.7 percent of the votes.)

Leader passed away in 1999, at the ripe old age of 17. After his death, Vincent ghost wrote *Follow the Leader: A Dog's Eye View of Washington, D.C.* by Leader Dole (Eastbank Publishing, 2000), with the proceeds going to WHS. The Doles, whose affection for Miniature Schnauzers continued unabated, adopted another Miniature Schnauzer puppy in 2000, whom they named Leader II. In memory of the original Leader, Vincent established the Leader Scholarship at KSU.

THE MINIATURE
IN MINIATURE

This mini-sized dog has a great big heart!

COUNTRY OF ORIGIN: Germany

WHAT HIS FRIENDS CALL HIM: Schnauzy, Beardy, Mini Mo, Pepper, The Big Schnauze

SIZE: stands up to 14 inches at the shoulder; weighs between 13 and 15 pounds

COAT & COLOR: The Mini's wiry coat is typically solid black or black and gray with silver-white trimmings around the face and on the feathered hair around the legs.

PERSONALITY TRAITS: This schnauzer is good-natured, friendly, devoted to his family and eager to please.

WITH KIDS: excellent with kids

WITH OTHER PETS: His amiable demeanor makes him compatible with other pets. He does like to chase small animals, though!

ENERGY LEVEL: high

EXERCISE NEEDS: Daily walks and lots of playtime are essential to curb his boisterous energy. Dog sports offer great exercise options.

GROOMING NEEDS: Weekly brushings will eliminate tangles, and regular grooming will maintain his snazzy schnauzer look.

TRAINING NEEDS: easy to train, a quick learner, simply needs basic obedience

LIVING ENVIRONMENT: The Miniature Schnauzer easily adapts to his surroundings and is suited to life in the city or country.

LIFESPAN: 12 to 14 years

A mere 150 years ago, the Miniature Schnauzer – at least as we know the breed today – didn't even exist. While certain 15th century German paintings show dogs that look similar to Miniature Schnauzers, these were likely smaller Standard Schnauzers, an established working dog, herder, hunter, guard dog and all-around farmhand well before anybody thought to create a smaller version of this stocky, wiry farmer's helper.

Considering the fact that the Miniature Schnauzer breed is a direct descendent of the Standard Schnauzer, it makes sense to begin by taking a quick look at the Miniature's big brother, so to speak, to more fully understand where the Miniature Schnauzer really began.

STANDARD BEGINNINGS

The Standard Schnauzer, or *Mittel-schnauzer* in German, is the oldest of the three schnauzers (Miniature and Giant being the other two). Originally called the Wire-Haired Pinscher, these dogs strongly resembled today's Standard Schnauzers and can be found in German artwork dating back as far

Did You Know? **The Mini is not as assertive as his bigger schnauzer cousins, but this rugged little dog can hold his own and will bark to sound the alarm.** Historically, the Mini served farmers as a ratter and partner by day and warmed the family's toes and hearts by night.

as the late 1300s. A statue from the 14th century stands in Mecklenborg, Germany, depicting a hunter with a schnauzer at his feet. Both Rembrandt and Durer painted schnauzers in various farm and village scenes, and Lucas Cranach included one in a tapestry dated 1501. The schnauzer was also the subject of a 1620 statue, "The Night Watchman" in Stuttgart, Germany. By the 1700s, schnauzers began to show up in the works of English artists, too.

But the schnauzers real champion was the European working class, which thought of the breed as a trusted all-around family dog. These sturdy, medium-sized, wire-haired working dogs, with their distinctive whiskers and game but loyal temperaments, were prized for hunting vermin in the field and guarding farmsteads at home and produce carts in town.

The word *schnauzer* (German for "snout") was first applied to the breed in 1842, and over the years it became synonymous with the Wire-Haired Pinscher. But during its early development, the breed was also known as the Rough-Haired Terrier, the *Rattenfanger* (rat catcher), the Wire-Haired German Pinscher and simply the Ratter.

Historians believe the breed was developed by mixing a spitz breed with the Dog of Bologne, the poodle, the Gray Wolf Spitz and the old German Pinscher stock. By 1850, the breed was recognized as pure and distinct, and Wire-Haired Pinschers were exhibited for the first time at the German International Show in Hanover in 1879. Although not as refined as the dogs of today, those early individuals exhibited the distinctive, shaggy facial hair; wiry double coats; elegantly arched necks; and cropped tails that remain the schnauzer's hallmarks today.

In 1880, German fanciers published the first breed standard for the "Wire-Haired German Pinscher, Ratter or Rat-catcher." The standard originally allowed for a wide variety of colors, including rust, tan, yellow and red. Then, in 1885, a German breeder named Hartenstein became interested in the black coat color and developed the Plavia line of black schnauzers, the beginning of the black color in these breeds. Five years later, G. Goller of Stuttgart, Germany, selectively bred reds to blacks to develop the pepper-and-salt color variation. Goller's foundation stock gave rise to what is now the dominant color in the breed. (Note: The other breeds refer to this color variation as pepper-and-salt.)

In that first decade after the standard was written, the breed began to evolve the elegant heads, heavy beards, prominent eyebrows and all-around breed type we have come to associate with the modern schnauzer breeds. During this period both the Miniature and Giant Schnauzers emerged.

Size reduction, in the Miniature's case, may have been achieved by introducing Affinpinscher and poodle blood while out-

it's a Fact

To create the Miniature Schnauzer, it is theorized the Standard Schnauzer may have been crossed with the Affenpinscher or Miniature Pinscher. Thus, he is still as high-spirited as the larger breeds, but he enjoys camaraderie with other dogs. When raised with children, the Mini makes a good playmate, though possibly a bit overwhelming for toddlers.

The Mini's distinct looks have been a long time in the making.

crosses to Great Danes and rough-coated shepherds achieved the larger, heavier frame of the Giant. Both retained the hunting skills and protective nature of the original breed, but the smaller dog could live more easily as a house pet. The Giant was pressed into service as a herder of cattle and sheep in the mountains of Bavaria, as well as a draft animal for pulling small carts and carrying loads of merchandise. Later, it would become a favorite breed for military and police work in both World Wars.

UNITED SCHNAUZERS OF AMERICA

Although the first Standard Schnauzer was said to have been shown in the Miscellaneous Class at the Westminster Kennel Club Dog Show in New York City in 1899, the breed was not imported seriously into the United States until after World War I. Many European immigrants brought their beloved working companions with them to the New World in the late 1800s, but the first official import was recorded in 1905, when a schnazuer named Fingal, bred by Goller, was imported by B. Leisching of Rochester, N.Y.

The Wire-Haired Pinscher Club of America was formed in 1925, and the club held its first specialty show two years later, with dogs classed in the American Kennel Club's Terrier Group. The original club included fanciers for Miniatures and Standards, but in 1933 the club divided each group to promote its breed separately. The name of the original parent club was changed to the Standard Schnauzer Club of America, and the Mini breed club took the name of American Miniature Schnauzer Club. (The Giant Schnauzer Club of America was formed in 1962.)

Up until the mid-1920s, schnauzers came in all colors, including black-and-tan, tricolor, fawn and cinnamon. But by the end of the decade, the solid black and the pepper-and-salt became the two most popular colors. Today, these are the only acceptable colors in Standard and Giant schnauzers.

THE MIGHTY MINIATURE

Miniature Schnauzers have become the most popular of the three schnauzer breeds in the United States, probably because their smaller size is more suited for urban life. The Mini is the only schnauzer to allow the color variation of black-and-silver, along with solid black and salt-and-pepper.

Although his features are that of a diminutive schnauzer, the Mini's attitude is more terrier-like, possibly due to the influence of the Affinpinscher which was used to reduce his size in the late 1800s. The Mini has been described as more laidback than a terrier, but with more spunk than his schnauzer cousin. Today's Mini breed standard calls for a terrier that is "alert and spirited, yet obedient to command."

Fanciers who appreciated the loyal, intelligent, game nature of the Standard Schnauzer wanted a smaller version that could hunt vermin both in the field and home. They kept the stocky build, wiry outer coat and distinctive

Just how quickly will your Miniature Schnauzer puppy grow? Go to Club Schnauzer and download a growth chart. You also can see your pup's age in human years. The old standard of multiplying your dog's age by seven isn't quite accurate. Log onto **DogChannel. com/Club-Schnauzer** and click on "Downloads."

A trait that is unique to schnauzers, and pretty much to most terriers, is their ratting instinct. While they want to please their owners, they cannot be left off leash in an unfenced area because if they see something they consider worth chasing, they will. Owners should never take them outside a fenced area without a leash because if they see a squirrel or bird, or even a bicyclist, rollerblader or roller-skater, they are inclined to chase. The breed was bred for this purpose.

— Michele Smith, rescue committee chairperson
of Chicago Miniature Schnauzer Club in Highland Park, Ill.

whiskers while reducing the size to between 12 and 14 inches at the shoulder.

Whether due to the Affinpinscher influence or selective breeding for the show ring, many of today's Miniature Schnauzers have lost the characteristic hard, wiry coat in favor of a softer, fluffier coat that lends itself more readily to the long, flowing locks favored by many judges.

The breed's U.S. beginnings trace back to 1924, when Marie Slattery imported four dogs from Germany to her Marienhof Kennel which became the foundation for the breed in the states. Almost all American-bred Minis descend from these four individuals. The AKC formally recognized the breed in 1926, and over the next 10 years, 108 imports arrived in America, mostly from Germany. In the early years, Minis were sometimes shown alongside the Standards, and both breeds shared the same parent club for the first decade.

When fanciers formed their own parent club (AMSC) in 1933, one of the breed's first winners was a salt-and-pepper male whelped in 1945 named Ch. Dorem Display. Bred by Dorothy Williams, Display led a long and productive life as a sire until his death in 1959. Many current winners trace back to him.

Although the breed standard allows the black-and-silver color, the color is recessive and was rel-

SMART TIP!

In a Mini whose outer coat is hand-stripped or plucked, the breed's double coat is maintained. Minis shown in conformation are always hand-stripped, never clipped, except for the head and private areas. Hand stripping, however, is a time-consuming process which requires the knowledge of which areas grow at a fast or slow rate. It is not just a matter of randomly pulling hairs. Those who show schnauzers usually strip their coats over three or four months, beginning with the area they want to be the longest when the dog is shown. To look its best, the Mini's coat should be either hand-stripped or clippered with its furnishings scissored to perfection, from its distinctive eyebrows to the flowing fullness of its cylindrical legs. With his sturdy good looks lending an almost military bearing to its appearance, balance is the groomer's goal in enhancing the Mini's sharp image.

The Mini's wiry coat has strayed from his larger counterparts to a softer, fluffier one.

and was relatively rare during the breed's development. The black-and-silver color variation is thought to come from the Affinpincher, and puppies are born black and tan, which gradually lightens to silver.

The majority of dogs in the Miniature ring are still salt-and-pepper, but blacks and black-and-silvers are no longer an oddity, both commanding respect from judges and breeders in their own right.

TERRIER TIES

In North America, a Miniature Schnauzer is considered a terrier, even if he doesn't share every trait with other terriers in his group, most of which come from Great Britain. "Their temperaments are, in a lot of ways, very similar to other terriers," says Wyoma Clouss of Boise, Idaho, who is the judges education chair for the American Miniature Schnauzer Club and an American Kennel Club-licensed terrier judge. They have the watchdog and rat-catcher-type temperaments."

But the big difference, Clouss says, is that Minis are more sensible. "That means they don't tend to be dog-aggressive like many other terriers," Clouss says. "You can have Miniature Schnauzers all together without fighting. They will bluff and carry on, but very rarely does a Miniature Schnauzer get into a serious fight with another dog."

While Miniature Schnauzers have a reputation as barkers, Clouss says the breed should not bark excessively and can be trained to tone it down. "They are not supposed to be yappy dogs," Clouss says. "A well-bred Miniature Schnauzer will bark to let you know something is going on, but they don't just bark at the moon." But, Clouss says, some lines do tend to bark more than others — just one more reason to get a good look at the parents of a litter of puppies before buying.

FULL CIRCLE

The schnauzer breeds originate in Germany, but their popularity has spread around the world. American breeders import and export to and from Hungary, Holland, Sweden, Australia, Japan, Russia, China and the Philippines. The appeal of a guard dog attitude in a house dog-sized package, combined with the good-natured temperament of a family dog, resonates with city dwellers far and near. Add in a small package in the in the Mini, and you might have the perfect dog.

For all that the Miniature Schnauzer is, his appeal and utility seem to cut across all barriers. They're the kind of dogs you'd want to go have a beer with down at the bar if they were people: dependable, unpretentious, honest and working-class dogs with a proud history of multiple uses.

NOTABLE & QUOTABLE *If you want a dog that is going to stop whatever he is doing and come straight to you the minute you speak, a schnauzer may not be the right breed for you. They have an independent side that some people may not care for. Another downside is that Miniature Schnauzers do not realize they are small. They will sometimes challenge a large dog, which can get them into much more trouble than they anticipated. — Mini owner Michelle Holland of Johnson City, Tenn.*

You have an unbreakable bond with your dog, but do you always understand him? Go online and download "Dog Speak," which outlines how dogs communicate. Find out what your Miniature Schnauzer is saying when he barks, howls or growls. Go to **DogChannel.com/Club-Schnauzer** and click on "Downloads."

Love in Miniature

What is it about Miniature Schnauzers that makes their owners love them so?

"Devotion," says Biff Atwater of Norfolk, Mass., proud owner of Tara, a 10-year-old black Mini. "They're just a wonderful-sized dog," adds his wife Mary. "You can pick them up and give them a hug, and they respond!"

Twelve-year-old Snafu, the pet of Alan and Sandra Hokanson, also of Norfolk, takes her job as a guard dog very seriously, especially when it comes to squirrels. "She hates them," Mr. Hokanson laughs. "She chases them up a tree, then she piddles on the spot where they were.

"She won't let anybody come in the yard, whether it's a person or an animal," he adds. Inside the house, she remains on duty. "When Sandy uses the bathroom, Snafu parks outside the door so no one else can go in."

"They don't shed," says Joy Christiansen of Norwood, Mass., owner of Libby, age 7. "We have allergy problems in our family. Their small size was also great when our kids were little, and at this stage of our lives, Libby is great with our grandchildren."

The breed's cleanliness was important to Reggie Butts of Walpole, Mass., owner of 9-year-old Kaiser. "They are hypoallergenic," he says. They also love to get up close and personal with their people. "Kaiser is like a big cat. He will crawl up and roll up in a ball beside you."

"Bradley is a very compassionate dog," observes Nancy Devito of her 7-year-old male. "He is very much a home dog. He never barks and he loves everybody." Residents of Plainville, Mass., the Devitos got their first schnauzer, Patrick, as a stray from the dog officer in a neighboring town. Seven weeks later, they were heartbroken when the previous owner spotted the dog with his new family reclaimed him. A canine custody battle ensued and the Devitos reluctantly returned him. Eighteen months later, the original owner contacted them and said he was theirs if they still wanted him.

"They said they couldn't handle him anymore," Devito recalls. "He was tearing up the house, eating their clothes, getting into chocolate. We had kept his bed, and we put it in the middle of the floor. He walked in the door and went right to it."

"They are just a smart, smart breed," adds Karen Doyle of Dedham, Mass., who has owned three of them. "When my mother and I were interviewed by the breeder, he told us they are a little dog with a human brain."

Although her pets have passed away, she still recalls how Teddy would bang on the back door to tell his owners he needed to go out. Heidi, his female predecessor, liked to dash outdoors for her morning potty run then jog right back upstairs to get back into bed.

Lisa Jo Mercado of Norfolk, Mass. was a professional dancer and instructor when she started researching prospective pets. "I had clients who were vets and some that showed different types of terri-ers," she recalls. "My biggest concern was that they'd be able to travel."

Now a busy mother of two, she and husband Jose have Shadow and Caesar, two 4-year-old schnauzers. "The best thing about these dogs is that they pick your spirits up. If you take care of them, they take care of you back," she maintains.

SELECTING A

SCHNAUZER

As rough and tumble as the Miniature Schnauzer can be, nothing is cuter than a little bearded schnauzer puppy. His sweet face and round little body inspire *oohs* and *ahhs* from all who see them. That wonderful endearing quality, however, can also distract you from taking the time and doing the legwork necessary to find a schnauzer puppy who's not only adorable but also healthy in body and temperament.

The key to finding the best Miniature Schnauzer puppy for you is to resist being charmed into a hasty decision and wait to find a responsible breeder. Then, you can have fun picking just the right puppy from a litter of those lovable faces.

You're going to have your Miniature Schnauzer for 12 to 14 years, so the time you spend early on to locate a healthy, well-adjusted puppy from a reputable breeder will definitely pay off in the long run. Look for a dedicated and ethical breeder who values good health and stable personalities, and who really cares what happens to the dog for the rest of his life.

> **Local breeder referrals are essential.** A breeder who belongs to a Miniature Schnauzer club shows active involvement in the breed, and breeds according to that particular club's code of ethics. That's who you want to do business with: a breeder who abides by a code of ethics.

it's a
Fact

Why is this so important? This is a breed with a unique personality who needs to be bred correctly by someone with experience who really knows what he or she is doing. If not, you may wind up with a dog who's overly aggressive, has a ton of health problems and doesn't even look like a Miniature Schnauzer.

Be sure to avoid puppy mills and backyard breeders. Puppy mills are large-scale breeding operations that produce puppies in an assembly-line fashion without regard to health and socialization. Backyard breeders are typically well-meaning, regular pet owners who simply do not possess enough knowledge about the breed and breeding to produce healthy puppies.

The American Kennel Club and the United Kennel Club provide a list of breeders in good standing with their organizations. Visit their websites, listed in the Resources chapter on page 166, for more information.

EVALUATING BREEDERS

Once you have the names and numbers of breeders in your area, start contacting them to find out more about their breeding programs. But, before you contact them, prepare some questions to ask that will get you the information you need to know.

Did You Know?

Good Breeder Signs
When you visit a Miniature Schnauzer breeder's home, look around the dwelling for:
- a clean, well-maintained facility
- no overwhelming odors
- an overall impression of cleanliness
- socialized dogs and puppies

Prospective buyers interview breeders much the same way that a breeder should interview a buyer. Make a list of questions and record the answers so you can compare them to the answers from other breeders whom you may interview later. The right questions are those that help you identify who has been in the breed a respectable number of years and who is actively showing their dogs. Ask in-depth questions regarding the genetic health of the parents, grandparents and great grandparents of any puppy you are considering. Ask what sort of genetic testing program the breeder adheres to.

You should look to see if a breeder actively shows his or her dogs in conformation events (aka dog shows). Showing indicates that the breeder is bringing out examples from his or her breeding program for the public to see. If there are any obvious problems, such as temperament or general conformation, they will be readily apparent. Also, the main reason to breed Miniature Schnauzers is to improve the quality of Miniature Schnauzers. If the breeder is not showing, then he or she is more likely to be breeding purely for the monetary aspect and may have less concern for the welfare and future of the breed.

Inquiring about health and determining the breeder's willingness to work with you in the future are also important for the potential puppy buyer to learn. The prospective buyer should see what kind of health guarantees the breeder gives. You should also find out if the breeder will be available for future consultation regarding your Miniature Schnauzer, and find out if the breeder will take your dog back if something unforeseen happens.

Prospective buyers should ask plenty of questions, and in return, buyers should also

Even if you want a pet-quality Miniature Schnauzer, go to a breeder who actively shows his or her dogs and choose a pup from a show-bred litter. You'll get a better puppy overall because this breeder will sincerely care about the future of the breed and focus on health, temperament and structure, rather than using the dogs to make extra money. — Mary Roberts, president of the Miniature Schnauzer Club of Birmingham, Ala.

be prepared to answer questions posed by a responsible breeder who wants to make sure his or her puppy is going to a good home. Be prepared for a battery of questions from the breeder regarding your purpose for wanting this breed of dog and whether you can properly care for one. Avoid buying from a breeder who does little or no screening. If a breeder doesn't ask any questions, they are not concerned with where their pups end up. In this case, the dogs' best interests are probably not the breeder's motive for breeding.

The buyer should find a breeder who is willing to answer any questions they have and are knowledgeable about the history of the breed, health issues and about the background of their own dogs. Learn about a breeder's long-term commitment to the Miniature Schnauzer breed and to his or her puppies after they leave the kennel.

Look for breeders who know their purpose for producing a particular litter, are knowledgeable in the pedigrees of their dogs and of the Miniature Schnauzer breed itself, and have had the necessary health screenings performed on the parents. They should also ask you for references to show that they are interested in establishing a relationship with you in consideration for a pup. If, after one phone conversation with a breeder, the person is supplying you with an address in which to send a deposit, continue your search for a reputable breeder elsewhere.

CHOOSING THE RIGHT PUP

Once you have found a breeder you are comfortable with, your next step is to pick the right puppy. The good news is that if you have done your homework and found a responsible breeder, you can count on this person to give you plenty of help in choosing the right pup for your personality and lifestyle. In fact, most good breeders will recommend a specific puppy once they know what kind of dog you want.

After you have narrowed down the search and selected a reputable breeder, rely on the experience of the breeder to help you select your puppy. The selection of the puppy depends a lot on what purpose the pup is being purchased for. If the puppy is being purchased as a show prospect, the breeder will offer his or her assessment of the pups that meet this criteria and be able to explain the strengths and faults of each pup.

Whether your Miniature Schnauzer puppy is show- or pet-quality, a good, stable temperament is vital for a happy relationship. Generally, you want to avoid a timid puppy or a very dominant one. Temperament is very important, and a reputable breeder should spend a lot of time with the pups and be able to offer an evaluation of each pup's personality.

A reputable breeder might tell you which Miniature Schnauzer puppy is appropriate for your home and personality. They may not allow you to choose the puppy, although they certainly will take your preference into consideration.

Questions to Expect

Be prepared for the breeder to ask you some questions, too.

This isn't a steadfast rule, and some breeders only insist on meeting the children to see how they handle puppies. It all depends on the breeder.

1. Have you previously owned a Miniature Schnauzer?

The breeder is trying to gauge how familiar you are with the breed. If you have never owned one, illustrate your knowledge of Miniature Schnauzers by telling the breeder about your research.

2. Do you have children? What are their ages?

Some breeders are wary about selling a dog to families with younger children.

3. How long have you wanted a Miniature Schnauzer?

This helps a breeder know if this purchase is an impulse buy or a carefully thought-out decision. Buying on impulse is one of the biggest mistakes owners can make. Be patient.

Join Club Schnauzer to get a complete list of questions a breeder should ask you. Click on "Downloads" at: **DogChannel.com/Club-Schnauzer**

Some breeders, on the other hand, believe it's important for you to be heavily involved in selecting a puppy from the litter. They will let their puppy buyers make the decision on which pup to take home because not everyone is looking for the same things in a dog. Some people want a quiet, laidback attitude. Others want an outgoing, active dog. When pups are old enough to go to their new homes at roughly 8 to 10 weeks of age, these breeders prefer you make your own decision because no one can tell at this age which pup will make the most intelligent or affectionate dog. The color, sex and markings are obvious, but that is about all you can tell for sure at this age. Everything else being equal — size, health, etc. — some breeders suggest picking the pup whom you have a gut feeling for.

The chemistry between a buyer and puppy is important and should play a role in determining which pup goes to which home. When possible, make numerous visits to see the puppies, and in effect, let a puppy choose you. There usually will be one puppy who spends more time with a buyer and is more comfortable relaxing and sitting with — or on — a person.

CHECKING FOR MINI QUALITIES

Whether you are dealing with a breeder who wants to pick a pup for you or lets you make the decision alone, consider certain points when evaluating the pup who you may end up calling your own. The puppy should be friendly and outgoing, not skittish in any way. He should be forgiving of correction. He shouldn't be too terribly mouthy. The pup should readily follow you and be willing to snuggle in your lap and be turned onto his back easily without a problem.

Proper temperament is very important. A Miniature Schnauzer puppy who has a dominant personality requires an experienced owner who will be firm during train-

With the popularity of Miniature Schnauzers, shelters and rescue groups across the country are often inundated with sweet, loving examples of the breed — from the tiniest puppies to senior dogs,

petite females to strapping males. Often, to get the schnauzer of your dreams, all it takes is a trip to the local shelter. Or, perhaps you can find your ideal dog waiting patiently in the arms of a foster parent at a nearby rescue group. It just takes a bit of effort, patience and a willingness to find the right dog for your family, not just the cutest dog on the block.

The perks of owning a Miniature Schnauzer are plentiful: companionship, unconditional love, true loyalty and laughter, just to name a few. So why choose the adoption option? Because you will literally be saving a life!

Owners of adopted dogs swear they're more grateful and loving than any dog they've owned before. It's almost as if they knew what dire fate awaited them, and are so thankful to you. Mini Schnauzers, known for their people-pleasing personalities, seem to embody this mentality wholeheartedly when they're rescued. And they want to give something back. Another perk: Almost all adopted dogs come fully vetted, with proper medical treatment, vaccinations, medicine, and most likely spayed or neutered. Some are even licensed and microchipped.

Don't disregard older dogs, thinking the only good pair-up is between you and a puppy. Adult schnauzers are more established behaviorally and personality-wise, helping to better mesh their characteristics with yours in this game of matchmaker. Puppies are always in high demand, so if you open your options to include adults, you will have a better chance of adopting quickly. Plus, adult dogs are often housetrained, more calm, chewproof and don't need to be taken outside in the middle of the night ... five times ... in the pouring rain.

The American Miniature Schnauzer Club offers rescue support information or log on to Petfinder.com. The site's searchable database enables you to find a Miniature Schnauzer in your area who needs a break in the form of a compassionate owner like you. More websites are listed in the Resources chapter on page 166.

WHY NOT RESCUE?

ing. A puppy who is a little shy requires heavy socialization to build his confidence.

You also can evaluate a Miniature Schnauzer puppy's temperament on your own. The temperament of the pups can be evaluated by spending some time watching them. If you can visit the pups and observe them first together with their littermates, then you can see how they interact with each other. You may be able to pinpoint which ones are the bullies and which ones are more submissive. In general, look for a puppy who is more interested in you than in his littermates. Then, take each pup individually to a new location away from the rest of the litter. Put the puppy down on the ground, walk away and see how he reacts away from the security of his littermates. The puppy may be afraid at first, but he should gradually recover and start checking out the new surroundings

D-I-Y TEMPERAMENT TEST

Puppies come in a wide assortment of temperaments to suit almost everyone. If you are looking for a dog who is easily trainable and a good companion to your family, you most likely want a puppy with a medium temperament.

Temperament testing can help you determine the type of disposition your potential puppy possesses. A pup with a medium temperament will have the following reactions to these various tests, best conducted when the pup is 7 weeks old.

Step 1. To test a pup's social attraction and his confidence in approaching humans, coax him toward you by kneeling down and clapping your hands gently. A pup with a medium temperament comes readily, tail up or down.

Step 2. To test a pup's eagerness to follow, walk away from him while he is watching you. He should follow you readily, tail up.

Step 3. To see how a pup handles restraint, kneel down and roll the pup gently on his back. Using a light but firm touch, hold him in this position with one hand for 30 seconds. The Miniature Schnauzer pup should

JOIN OUR ONLINE **Club Schnauzer**™

Breeder Q&A

Here are some questions you should ask a breeder and the answers you want.

Q. How often do you have litters available?

A. You want to hear "once or twice a year" or "occasionally" because a breeder who doesn't have litters that often is probably more concerned with the quality of his puppies, rather than with making money.

Q. What kinds of health problems do schnauzers have?

A. Beware of a breeder who says, "none." Every breed has health issues. For Miniature Schnauzers, some health problems include allergies, diabetes, cataracts and urinary stones.

Get a complete list of questions to ask a Miniature Schnauzer breeder — and the correct answers — at Club Miniature Schnauzer. Log onto **DogChannel.com/Club-Schnauzer** and click on "Downloads."

settle down after some initial struggle and offer some or steady eye contact.

Step 4. To evaluate a puppy's level of social dominance, stand up, then crouch down beside the pup and stroke him from head to back. A schnauzer puppy with a medium temperament — neither too dominant nor too submissive — should cuddle up to you and lick your face, or squirm and lick your hands.

Step 5. An additional test of a pup's dominance level is to bend over, cradle the pup under his belly with your fingers interlaced and palms up, and elevate him just off the ground. Hold him there for 30 seconds. The pup should not struggle and should be relaxed, or he should struggle and then settle down and lick you.

PHYSICAL FEATURES

To assess each puppy's health, take a deliberate, thorough look at each part of his body. Signs of a healthy puppy include bright eyes, a healthy coat, a good appetite and firm stool.

Watch for a telltale link between physical and mental health. A healthy Mini Schnauzer, as with any breed of puppy, will display a happier, more positive attitude

than an unhealthy puppy. A Miniature Schnauzer puppy's belly should not be over extended or hard, as this may be a sign of worms. Also, if you are around the litter long enough to witness a bowel movement, the stool should be solid, and the pup should not show any signs of discomfort. Look into the pup's eyes, too; they should be bright and full of life.

Newborns get their immunities from their mother. As they grow, they'll depend on you.

PUPPY PARTICULARS

Here are signs to look for when picking a Mini Schnauzer puppy from a breeder. When in doubt, ask the breeder which puppy they think has the best personality/temperament to fit your lifestyle.

1. Look at the area where the pups spend most of their time. It's OK if they play outdoors part of the day, but they should sleep indoors at night so the pups can interact with people and become accustomed to hearing ordinary household noises. This builds a solid foundation for a well-socialized and secure Miniature Schnauzer puppy. The puppies' area should be clean, well lit, have fresh drinking water and interesting toys.

2. Sure, you're only buying one Mini Schnauzer puppy, but make sure to see all of the puppies in the litter. By 5 weeks of age, healthy pups will begin playing with one another and should be lively and energetic. It's OK if they're asleep when you visit, but stay long enough to see them wake up. Once they're up, they shouldn't be lethargic or weak, as this may be a sign of illness.

3. Pups should be confident and eager to greet you. A puppy who is shy or fearful and stays in the corner may be sick or insecure. Although some introverted pups come out of their shells later on, many do not. These dogs will always be fearful as adults and are not good choices for an active family with or without children, or for people who have never had a dog before. They frighten easily and will require a lot of training and socialization in order to live a happy life.

Choose a pup who is happy and eager to interact with you but reject the one who is either too shy or too bossy. These temperament types are a challenge to deal with, and require a tremendous amount of training to socialize. The perfect Miniature Schnauzer puppy personality is somewhere between the two extremes.

4. If it's feeding time during your visit, all pups should be eager to gobble up their food. A puppy who refuses to eat may signal illness.

5. The dog's skin should be smooth, clean and shiny without any sores or bumps. Puppies should not be biting or scratching at themselves continuously, which could signal fleas.

6. After 10 to 12 days, eyes should be open and clear without any redness or discharges. Pups should not be scratching at their eyes, as this may cause an infection or be a sign irritation.

7. Vomiting or coughing more than once is not normal. If this happens, a Mini puppy might be ill and should visit the vet immediately.

8. Visit long enough to see the Miniature Schnauzer pups eliminate. All stools should be firm without being watery or bloody. These are signs of illness or that a puppy has worms.

9. Miniature Schnauzer puppies should walk or run freely without limping.

10. A healthy Miniature Schnauzer puppy who is getting enough to eat should not be skinny. You should be able to slightly feel his ribs if you rub his abdomen, but you should not be able to see protruding ribs.

BREEDER PAPERS

Everything today comes with an instruction manual. When you purchase a Miniature Schnauzer puppy, it's no different. A reputable breeder should give you a registration application; a sales contract; a health guarantee; your puppy's complete health records; a three-, four- or five-generation pedigree; and some general information on behavior, care, conformation, health and training.

Registration Application. This document from the AKC or UKC assigns your puppy a number and identifies the dog by listing his date of birth, the names of the parents and shows that he is registered as a purebred Mini. It doesn't prove whether or not your dog is a show- or pet-quality Miniature Schnauzer and doesn't provide any health guarantee.

Sales Contract. A reputable breeder should discuss the terms of the contract with you before asking you to sign it. This is a written understanding of both of your expectations and shows that the breeder cares about the pup's welfare throughout his life. The contract can require you to keep the dog indoors at night, spay or neuter if the puppy is not going to be a show dog, and provide routine vet care and assurance that you'll feed your dog a healthy diet. Most responsible breeders will ask that you take your dog to obedience classes and earn a Canine Good Citizen title (an AKC training certification for dogs that exhibit good manners) before he is

2 years old. Many breeders also require new owners to have totally secure fencing and gates around their yard. Schnauzers can be incredible escape artists, and they will find a way out of the yard if there's even the slightest opening.

Make sure your pup has been vaccinated properly before you take him out on socializing adventures.

Health Guarantee. This includes a letter from a veterinarian that the puppy has been examined and is healthy, and states that the breeder will replace your dog if he were to develop a genetic, life-threatening illness during his lifetime.

Health Records. Here's everything you want to know about your puppy's and his parents' health. It should include the dates the puppy was vaccinated, dewormed and examined by a veterinarian for signs of heart murmur, plus the parents' test results for the presence or absence of hip and elbow dysplasia, heart problems and luxated patellas.

Pedigree. Breeders should provide you with a copy of the puppy's three-, four- or five-generation pedigree. Many breeders also have photos of the dog's ancestors that they will proudly share with you.

A curious puppy that wants to investigate you is a good sign.

Extra Information. The best breeders pride themselves on giving new owners a notebook full of the latest information about Miniature Schnauzer behavior, care, conformation, health and training. Be sure to read it because it will provide valuable help while raising your Miniature Schnauzer.

Healthy Puppy Signs

Here are a few things you should look for when selecting a puppy from a litter.

1. NOSE: It should be slightly moist to the touch, but there shouldn't be excessive discharge. The puppy should persistently not be sneezing or sniffling.

2. SKIN AND COAT: Your schnauzer puppy's coat should be soft and shiny, without flakes or excessive shedding. Watch out for patches of missing hair, redness, bumps or sores. The pup should have a pleasant smell. Check for parasites, such as fleas or ticks.

3. BEHAVIOR: A healthy schnauzer pup may be sleepy, but he should not be lethargic. He will be playful at times, not isolated in a corner. You should also see occasional bursts of energy and interaction with littermates. When it's mealtime, a healthy puppy will take an interest in his food.

There are more signs to look for when picking out the perfect Mini puppy for your lifestyle. Download the list at **DogChannel.com/Club-Schnauzer**

All schnauzer puppies are cute, but a smart owner will wait to purchase theirs until they find the right breeder and puppy.

ESSENTIALS

Don't for one second think that a Miniature Schnauzer would prefer to live in a miniature area outside! He, like every other breed, wants to live in the best accommodations with plenty of toys, soft bedding and other luxuries. Your home is now his home, too; and, before you even bring that new puppy or rescue dog into his new forever home, be a smart owner and make your home accessible for him.

In fact, in order for him to grow into a stable, well-adjusted dog, he has to feel comfortable in his surroundings. Remember, he is leaving the warmth and security of his mother and littermates, as well as the familiarity of the only place he has ever known, so it is important to make his transition to your home — his new home — as easy as possible.

PUPPY-PROOFING

Aside from making sure that your Miniature Schnauzer will be comfortable in your home, you also have to ensure that your home is safe, which means taking the proper precautions to keep your pup away from things that are dangerous for him.

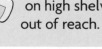

it's a **Fact**

Dangers lurk indoors and outdoors. Keep your curious schnauzer from investigating your shed and garage. Antifreeze and fertilizers, such as those you would use for roses, can kill any dog. Keep these items on high shelves that are out of reach.

A well-stocked toy box should contain three main categories of toys.
1. **action** — anything that you can throw or roll and get things moving
2. **distraction** — durable toys that make dogs work for a treat
3. **comfort** — soft, stuffed "security blankets"

Puppy-proof your home inside and out before bringing your Miniature Schnauzer home for the first time. Place breakables out of reach. If he is limited to certain places within the house, keep potentially dangerous items in off-limit areas. If your Miniature Schnauzer is going to spend time in a crate, make sure that there isn't anything near it that he can reach if he sticks his curious little nose or paws through the openings.

The outside of your home must also be safe. Your pup will want to run and explore the yard, and he should be granted that freedom — as long as you are there to supervise. Do not let a fence give you a false sense of security; you would be surprised how crafty and persistent a Miniature Schnauzer puppy can be in figuring out how to dig under a fence or squeeze his way through holes. The remedy is to make the fence well embedded into the ground. Be sure to repair or secure any gaps in the fence. Check the fence periodically to ensure that it is in good shape and make repairs as needed; a very determined puppy may work on the same spot until he is able to get through.

The following are a few common problem areas to watch out for in the home.

■ **Electrical cords and wiring:** No electrical cord or wiring is safe. Many office-supply stores sell products to keep wires gathered under computer desks, as well as products that prevent office chair wheels (and puppy teeth) from damaging electrical cords. If you have exposed cords and wires, these products aren't very expensive and can be used to keep a puppy out of trouble.

■ **Trash cans:** Don't waste your time trying to train your Miniature Schnauzer not to get into the trash. Simply put the garbage behind a cabinet door and use a child-safe lock, if necessary. Dogs love bathroom trash, which consists of items that can be

A smart owner will make their Miniature Schnauzer feel safe and comfortable at home.

extremely dangerous (i.e., cotton balls, cotton swabs, used razors, dental floss, etc.)! Put the bathroom trash can in a cabinet under the sink and make sure you always shut the door to the bathroom.

■ **Household cleaners:** Make sure your Miniature Schnauzer puppy doesn't have access to any of these deadly chemicals. Keep them behind closed cabinet doors, using child-safe locks, if necessary.

■ **Pest control sprays and poisons:** Chemicals to control ants or other pests should never be used in the house, if possible. Your Miniature Schnauzer pup doesn't have to directly ingest these poisons to become ill; if he steps in the poison, he can experience toxic effects by licking his paws. Roach motels and other toxic pest traps are also yummy to dogs, so don't drop these behind couches or cabinets; if there's room for a roach motel, there's room for a determined Miniature Schnauzer.

■ **Fabric:** Here's one you might not think about: Some puppies have a habit of licking blankets, upholstery, rugs or carpets. Though this habit seems fairly innocuous, over time the fibers from the upholstery or carpet can accumulate in the dog's stomach and cause a blockage. If you see your dog licking these items, remove the item or prevent him from having contact with it.

■ **Prescriptions, painkillers, supplements and vitamins:** Keep all medications in a cabinet. Also, be very careful when taking your prescription medications, supplements or vitamins: How often have you

dropped a pill? You can be sure that your schnauzer puppy will be between your legs and will snarf up the pill before you even start to say "No!" Dispense your own pills carefully and without your MIni present.

■ **Miscellaneous loose items:** If it's not bolted to the floor, your puppy is likely to give the item a taste test. Socks, coins, children's toys, game pieces, cat toys — you name it. If it's on the floor, it's worth a try. Make sure the floors in your home are picked up and free of clutter.

FAMILY INTRODUCTIONS

Everyone in the house will be excited about the puppy's homecoming and will want to pet and play with him, but it is best to make the introduction low-key so as not to overwhelm your puppy. He will already be apprehensive. It is the first time he has been separated from his mother, littermates and breeder, and the ride to your home is likely to be the first time he has been in a car. The last thing you want to do is smother your Miniature Schnauzer pup, as this will only frighten him further. This is not to say that human contact is unnecessary at this stage because this is the time when a connection between the pup and his human family is formed. Gentle petting and soothing words should help console your Miniature Schnauzer, as well as putting him down and letting him explore on his own (under your watchful eye, of course).

Your pup may approach the family members or may busy himself with exploring for

JOIN OUR
ONLINE
Club
Schnauzer™
Before you bring your Miniature Schnauzer home, make sure you don't have anything that can put her in harm's way. Go to Club Schnauzer and download a list of poisonous plants and foods to avoid. Log on to **DogChannel.com/Club-Schnauzer** and click on "Downloads."

The first thing you should always do before your puppy comes home is to lie on the ground and look around. You want to be able to see everything your puppy is going to see. For the puppy, the world is one big chew toy.

— Cathleen Stamm, rescue volunteer in San Diego, Calif.

a while. Gradually, each person should spend some time with the pup, one at a time, crouching down to get as close to your Miniature Schnauzer's level as possible, letting him sniff their hands before petting him gently. He definitely needs human attention, and he needs to be touched; this is how to form an immediate bond. Just remember that the pup is experiencing a lot of things for the first time, all at once. There are new people, new noises, new smells and new things to investigate. Be gentle, be affectionate and be as comforting as you possibly can be.

PUP'S FIRST NIGHT HOME

You have traveled home with your new puppy safely in his crate. He may have already been to the vet for a thorough check-

If you aren't going to get involved in conformation (dog shows), have your male Mini neutered. He'll be more calm and better behaved, and it'll help control the pet population.

up — he's been weighed, his papers examined, perhaps he's even been vaccinated and dewormed. Your Miniature Schnauzer has met and licked the whole family, including the excited children and the less-than-happy cat. He's explored his area, his new bed, the yard and everywhere else he's permitted. He's eaten his first meal at home and relieved himself in

SMART TIP!

When you are unable to watch your Miniature Schnauzer puppy, put her in a crate or an exercise pen on an easily cleanable floor. If she has an accident on carpeting, clean it completely and meticulously, so that it doesn't smell like her potty forever.

All pet females should be spayed. Not only will they not get pregnant, but it will lower some cancer risks.

the proper place. Your Miniature Schnauzer has heard lots of new sounds, smelled new friends and seen more of the outside world than ever before. This was just the first day! He's worn out and is ready for bed — or so you think!

Remember, this is your puppy's first night to sleep alone. His mother and littermates are no longer at paw's length, and he's scared, cold and lonely. Be reassuring to your new family member. This is not the time to spoil your Miniature Schnauzer and give in to his inevitable whining.

Puppies whine. They whine to let others know where they are and hopefully to get company out of it. Place your Miniature Schnauzer puppy in his new bed or crate in his room and close the door. Mercifully, he may fall asleep without a peep. If the inevitable occurs, ignore the whining; he is fine. Do not give in and visit your Miniature Schnauzer puppy. He will fall asleep eventually.

Many breeders recommend placing a piece of bedding from his former home in his new bed so that he will recognize the scent of his littermates. Others still advise placing a hot water bottle in his bed for warmth. The latter may be a good idea provided the pup doesn't attempt to suckle.

Your Miniature Schnauzer's first night can be somewhat terrifying for him. Remember that you set the tone of nighttime at your house. Unless you want to play with your Mini puppy every night at 10 p.m., midnight and 2 a.m., don't initiate the habit. Your family will thank you, and so will your pup!

PET-SUPPLY STORE SHOPPING

It's fun shopping for new things for a new puppy. From training to feeding and sleeping to playing, your new Miniature

Schnauzer will need a few items to make life comfy, easy and fun. Be prepared and visit your local pet-supply store before you bring home your new family member.

◆ **Collar and ID tag:** Acclimate your dog to wearing a collar the first day you bring him home. Not only will a collar and ID tag help your puppy in the event that he becomes lost, but collars are also an important training tool. If your Miniature Schnauzer gets into trouble, the collar will act as a handle, helping you divert him to a more appropriate behavior. Make sure the collar fits snugly enough so that your schnauzer cannot wriggle out of it, but is loose enough so that it will not be uncomfortably tight around his neck. You should be able to fit a finger between your pup's neck and the collar. Collars come in many styles, but for starting out, a simple buckle collar with an easy-release snap works great.

◆ **Leash:** For training or just for taking a stroll down the street, a leash is your Miniature Schnauzer's vehicle to explore the outside world. Like collars, leashes come in a variety of styles and materials. A 6-foot

NOTABLE & QUOTABLE

Playing with toys from puppyhood encourages good behavior and social skills throughout your dog's life. A happy, playful dog is a content and well-adjusted one. Also, because all puppies chew to soothe their gums and help loosen puppy teeth, dogs should always have easy access to several different toys.

— dog trainer and author Harrison Forbes of Savannah, Tenn.

SMART TIP!

Keep a crate in your vehicle and take your schnauzer along when you visit the drive-thru at the bank or your favorite fast-food restaurant. She can watch interactions, hear interesting sounds and maybe earn a dog treat.

nylon leash is a popular choice because it is lightweight and durable. As your pup grows and gets used to walking on the leash, you may want to purchase a flexible leash. These leads allow you to extend the length to give your dog a broader area to explore or to shorten the length to keep your dog closer to you.

◆ **Bowls:** Your Miniature Schnauzer will need two bowls: one for water and one for food. You may want two sets of bowls, one for inside and one for outside, depending on where your dog will be fed and where he will be spending time. Bowls should be sturdy enough so that they don't tip over easily. (Most have reinforced bottoms that prevent tipping.) Bowls are usually made of metal, ceramic or plastic, and should be easy to clean.

◆ **Crate:** A multipurpose crate serves as a bed, housetraining tool and travel carrier. It also is the ideal doggie den — a bedroom of sorts — that your Miniature Schnauzer can retire to when he wants to rest or just needs a break. The crate should be large enough for your dog to stand in, turn around and lie down. You don't want any more room than this — especially if you're planning on using the crate to housetrain your dog — because he will eliminate in one corner and lie down in another. Get a crate that is big enough for your dog when

The more cluttered your house, the more there is for your Mini to get into. Keep you house as clutter-free as possible to keep everyone happy and healthy.

he is an adult. Then, use dividers to limit the space when he's a puppy.

◆ **Bed:** A plush doggie bed will make sleeping and resting more comfortable for your Miniature Schnauzer. Dog beds come in all shapes, sizes and colors, but your dog just needs one that is soft and large enough for him to stretch out on. Because puppies and rescue dogs may not always be housetrained, it's helpful to buy a bed that can be easily washed. If your Miniature Schnauzer will be sleeping in a crate, a nice crate pad and a small blanket that he can burrow in will help him feel more at home. Replace the blanket if it becomes ragged and starts to fall apart because your Miniature Schnauzer's nails could get caught in it.

◆ **Gate:** Similar to those used for toddlers, gates help keep your Mini Schnauzer

confined to one room or area when you can't supervise him. Gates also work well to keep your schnauzer out of areas you don't want him in. Gates are available in many types and styles. Make sure you choose one with openings small enough so your Mini puppy can't squeeze through the bars or any gaps.

Dogs don't understand "sometimes." If you don't want your Mini on the furniture, don't allow it on "special occasions." Be consistent and your Mini will learn the house rules.

◆ **Toys:** Keep your dog occupied and entertained by providing him with an array of fun toys. Teething puppies like to chew — in fact, chewing is a physical need for pups as they are teething — and everything from your shoes to the leather couch to the fancy rug are fair game. Divert your Miniature Schnauzer's chewing instincts with durable toys like bones made of nylon or hard rubber.

Other fun toys include rope toys, treat-dispensing toys and balls. Make sure the toys and bones don't have small parts that could break off and be swallowed, causing your dog to choke. Stuffed toys can become destuffed, and an overly excited Mini puppy may ingest the stuffing or the squeaker. Check your Miniature Schnauzer's toys regularly and replace them if they become frayed or show signs of wear.

◆ **Cleaning supplies:** Until your Miniature Schnauzer puppy is house-trained, you will be doing a lot of cleaning. Accidents will occur, which is acceptable in the beginning because the puppy doesn't know any better. All you can do is be pre-

Funny Bone

To err is human; to forgive, canine.

— *Anonymous*

pared to clean up any accidents. Old rags, towels, newspapers and a stain-and-odor remover are good to have on hand.

BEYOND THE BASICS

The basic items discussed in this chapter are the bare necessities. You will find out what else you and your new schnauzer need as you both go along — grooming supplies, flea/tick protection — and these things will vary depending on your situation. It is important, however, that you have everything you need to make your Miniature Schnauzer comfortable in his new home. So start shopping!

Some ordinary household items make great toys for your schnauzer — as long you make sure they are safe. Tennis balls, plastic water bottles, old towels and more can be transformed into fun with a little creativity. You can find a list of homemade toys at **DogChannel.com/Club-Schnauzer**

JOIN OUR
ONLINE
**Club
Schnauzer**™

SUCCESSFUL

HOUSETRAINING

Unexciting as it may be, the house-training part of puppy rearing greatly affects the budding relationship between a smart owner and his puppy — particularly when it becomes an area of ongoing contention. Fortunately, armed with suitable knowledge, patience and common sense, you'll find housetraining progresses at a relatively smooth rate. That leaves more time for the important things, like cuddling your adorable puppy, showing him off and laughing at his high jinks.

The answer to successful housetraining is total supervision and management — crates, tethers, exercise pens and leashes — until you know your dog has developed preferences for outside surfaces (grass, gravel, concrete) instead of carpet, tile or hardwood, and knows that potty happens outside.

IN THE BEGINNING

For the first two to three weeks of a puppy's life, his mother helps the pup to eliminate. The mother also keeps the whelping box or "nest area" clean. When pups begin to walk around and eat on their own, they choose where they eliminate. You can train your puppy to relieve himself wherever

it's a **Fact** **Ongoing housetraining difficulties may indicate your pup has a health problem,** warranting a vet check. A urinary infection, parasites, a virus and other nasty issues greatly affect your puppy's ability to hold pee or poop.

you choose, but this must be somewhere suitable. You should bear in mind from the outset that when your puppy is old enough to go out in public places, you must be considerate and pick up after him. You will always have to carry with you a small plastic bag or poop scoop.

Outdoor training includes such surfaces as grass, soil and concrete. Indoor training usually means training your dog on newspaper. When deciding on the surface and location that you will want your Miniature Schnauzer to use, be sure it is going to be permanent. Training your dog on grass and then changing two months later is extremely difficult for dog and owner.

Next, choose the cue you will use each and every time you want your puppy to eliminate. "Let's go," "hurry up" and "potty" are examples of cues commonly used by smart dog owners.

Get in the habit of giving your puppy the chosen relief cue before you take him out. That way, when he becomes an adult, you will be able to determine if he wants to go out when you ask him. A confirmation will be signs of interest, such as wagging his tail, watching you intently or going to the door.

LET'S START WITH THE CRATE

Clean animals by nature, dogs dislike soiling where they sleep and eat. This fact makes a crate a useful tool for housetraining. When purchasing a new crate, consider that an appropriately sized crate will allow adequate room for an adult Miniature Schnauzer to stand full-height, lie on his side without scrunching and turn around easily. If debating plastic versus wire crates, short-haired breeds sometimes prefer the warmer, draft-blocking quality of plastic, while furry dogs often like the cooling airflow of a wire crate.

Some crates come with a movable wall that reduces the interior size to provide enough space for your puppy to stand, turn and lie down, while not allowing him room to soil one end and sleep in the other. The problem is that if your puppy goes potty in the crate anyway, the divider forces him to lie in his own excrement.

This can work against you by desensitizing your puppy against his normal, instinctive revulsion to resting where he has just eliminated. If scheduling permits you or a responsible family member to clean the crate soon after it's soiled, then you can continue to cratetrain because limiting crate size does encourage your puppy to hold it. Otherwise, give him enough room to move away from an unclean area until he's better able to control his elimination.

Needless to say, not every Miniature Schnauzer puppy adheres to this guideline. If your Miniature Schnauzer moves along at a faster pace, thank your lucky stars. Should he progress slower, accept it and remind yourself that he'll improve. Be aware that puppies frequently hold it longer at night than during the day. Just because your puppy sleeps for six or more hours through the night, it does not mean he can hold it that long during the more active daytime hours.

One last bit of advice on the crate: Place it in the corner of a high-traffic room, such as the family room or kitchen. Social and

Don't let a stubborn
schnauzer get you down.
Be patient and consistent.

Take your schnauzer to the same potty spot each trip. That way, he'll know where it is appropriate to potty.

curious by nature, dogs like to feel included in family happenings. Creating a quiet retreat by putting the crate in an unused area may seem like a good idea, but results in your puppy feeling insecure and isolated. Watching his people pop in and out of the crate room reassures your puppy that he's not forgotten.

A PUP'S GOT NEEDS

Your puppy needs to relieve himself after play periods, after each meal, after he has been sleeping and any time he indicates that he is looking for a place to urinate or defecate.

The urinary and intestinal tract muscles of very young puppies are not fully developed. Therefore, like human babies, puppies need to relieve themselves frequently. Take your puppy out often — every hour for an 8-week-old, for example — and always immediately after sleeping and eating. The older the puppy, the less often he will need to relieve himself. Finally, as a mature, healthy adult, he will require only three to five relief trips per day.

HOUSING HELPS

Because the types of housing and control you provide for your Miniature Schnauzer

How often does a Miniature Schnauzer puppy do his business?
A lot! Go to **DogChannel.com/Club-Schnauzer** and download the typical peeing and pooping schedule of a puppy. You can also download a chart that you can fill out to track your dog's elimination timetable, which will help you with housetraining.

JOIN OUR ONLINE Club Schnauzer™

NOTABLE & QUOTABLE

Reward your pup with a high-value treat immediately after he potties to reinforce going in the proper location, then play for a short time afterward. This teaches that good things happen after pottying outside! — Victoria Schade, certified pet dog trainer, from Annandale, Va.

SMART TIP!

If you acquire your Miniature Schnauzer puppy at 8 weeks of age, expect to take her out at least six to eight times a day. By the time she's about 6 months old, potty trips will be down to three or four times a day. A rule of thumb is to take your puppy out in hourly intervals equal to her age in months.

puppy have a direct relationship on the success of housetraining, you must consider the various aspects of both before beginning training. Taking a new puppy home and turning him loose in your house can be compared to turning a child loose in a sports arena and telling the child that the place is all his! The sheer enormity of the place would be too much for him to handle. Instead, offer the puppy clearly defined areas where he can play, sleep, eat and live. A room of the house where the family gathers is the most obvious choice.

Puppies are social animals and need to feel like they are a part of the pack right from the start. Hearing your voice, watching you while you are doing things and smelling you nearby are all positive reinforcers that he is now a member of your pack. Usually a family room, the kitchen or a nearby adjoining breakfast area is ideal for providing safety and security for puppy and owner.

Within that room, there should be a smaller area that your Miniature Schnauzer puppy can call his own. An alcove, a wire or fiberglass dog crate, or a fenced (not boarded!) corner from which he can view the activities of his new family will be fine. The designated area should be lined with clean bedding and a toy. Water must always be available, in a nonspill container, once your dog is housetrained.

IN CONTROL

By control, we mean helping your puppy to create a lifestyle pattern that will be compatible to that of his human pack (you!). Just as we guide children to learn our way of life, we must show our Miniature Schnauzer pup when it is time to play, eat, sleep, exercise and entertain himself.

Your puppy should always sleep in his crate. He should also learn that, during times of household confusion and excessive human activity, such as at breakfast when family members are preparing for the day, he can play by himself in relative safety and comfort in his designated area. Each time you leave your Miniature Schnauzer alone, he should understand exactly where he is supposed to stay.

Other times of excitement, such as family parties, can be fun for your puppy, provided that he can view the activities from the security of his designated area. He is not underfoot, and he is not being fed all sorts of tidbits that will probably cause him stomach distress, yet he still feels a part of the fun.

Puppies are chewers. They cannot tell the difference between lamp cords, television wires, shoes or table legs. Chewing into a television wire, for example, can be fatal to the puppy, while a shorted wire can start a fire in the house.

If the puppy chews on the arm of the chair when he is alone, you probably will discipline him angrily when you get home. Thus, he makes the association that your coming home means he is going to be punished. (He will not remember chewing the chair and is incapable of making the association of the discipline with his naughty deed.)

Reward a good potty with plenty of praise.

Having housetraining problems with your schnauzer? Ask other Miniature Schnauzer owners for advice and tips, or post your own success story to give other owners encouragement. Log onto **DogChannel.com/Club-Schnauzer** and click on "Community."

When proximity prevents you from going home at lunch or during periods when overtime crops up, make alternative arrangements for getting your puppy out. Hire a pet-sitting or walking service, or enlist the aid of an obliging neighbor.

SCHEDULE A SOLUTION

A puppy should be taken to his relief area each time he is released from his designated area, after meals, after play sessions and when he first awakens in the morning (at 8 weeks of age, this can mean 5 a.m.!). The puppy will indicate that he's ready "to go" by circling or sniffing busily — do not misinterpret these signs. For a puppy less than 10 weeks of age, a routine of taking him out every hour is necessary. As your puppy grows, he will be able to wait for longer periods of time.

Keep potty trips to your puppy's relief area short. Stay no more than 5 or 6 minutes, and then return to inside the house. If your puppy potties during that time, lavishly praise him and then immediately take him indoors. If he does not potty, but he has an accident later when you go back indoors, pick him up, say "No! No!" and return to his relief area. Wait a few minutes, then return to the house again. Never hit your Miniature Schnauzer puppy or rub his face in urine or excrement when he has had an accident.

Once indoors, put your puppy in his crate until you have had time to clean up his accident. Then release him to the family area and watch him more closely than before. Chances are, his accident was a result of your not picking up his potty signals or waiting too long before offering him the opportunity to relieve himself. Never hold a grudge against your puppy for accidents.

Let your puppy learn that going outdoors means it is time to relieve himself, not to play.

Make sure potty time is not mistaken for play time.

Did You Know? White vinegar is a good odor remover if you don't have any professional cleaners on hand; use one-quarter cup vinegar to one quart of water.

Each time you put your puppy in his own area, use the same cue, whatever suits you best. Soon, he will run to his crate or special area when he hears you say those words. Remember that one of the primary ingredients in housetraining your puppy is control. There will always be occasions when you will need to have a place where your dog can be happy and safe. Cratetraining is the answer for now and in the future.

A few key elements are really all you need to create a successful housetraining method: consistency, frequency, praise, control and supervision. By following these simple procedures with a normal, healthy puppy, you and your Miniature Schnauzer will soon be past the stage of accidents and ready to move on to a full and rewarding life together.

Once trained, he will be able to play indoors and outdoors and still differentiate between the times for play versus the times for relief.

Help him develop regular hours for naps, being alone, playing by himself and just resting — all in his crate. Encourage him to entertain himself while you are busy elsewhere. Let him learn that having you nearby is comforting, but it is not your main purpose in life to provide him with undivided attention.

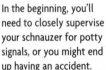

In the beginning, you'll need to closely supervise your schnauzer for potty signals, or you might end up having an accident.

10 HOUSETRAINING HOW-TOS

1. Decide where you want your schnauzer to eliminate. Take her there every time until she gets the idea. Pick a spot that's easy to access. Remember, puppies have very little time between "gotta go" and "oops."

2. Teach an elimination cue, such as "go potty" or "get busy." Say this every time you take your Miniature Schnauzer to eliminate. Don't keep chanting the cue; just say it once or twice, and then keep quiet so you won't distract your dog.

3. Praise calmly when your dog eliminates, but stand there a little longer in case there's more.

4. Keep potty outings for potty only. Take your dog to the designated spot, tell her "go potty" and just stand there. If she needs to eliminate, she will do so within five minutes.

5. Don't punish for potty accidents; punishment can hinder progress. If you catch your schnauzer in the act indoors, verbally interrupt but don't scold. Gently carry or lead your pup to the approved spot, let her finish, then praise.

6. If it's too late to interrupt an accident, scoop the poop or blot up the urine afterward with a paper towel. Immediately take your dog and her deposit (gently!) to the potty area. Place the poop or trace of urine on the ground and praise the pup. If she sniffs at her waste, praise more. Let your schnauzer know you're pleased when her waste is in the proper area.

7. Keep track of when and where your schnauzer eliminates — that will help you anticipate potty times. Regular meals mean regular elimination, so feed your dog scheduled, measured meals instead of free feeding (leaving food available at all times).

8. Hang a bell on a sturdy cord from the doorknob. Before you open the door to take your puppy out for potty, shake the string and ring the bell. Most dogs soon realize the connection between the bell ringing and the door opening, then they'll try it out for themselves.

9. Dogs naturally return to re-soil where they've previously eliminated, so thoroughly clean up all accidents. Household cleaners will usually do the job, but special enzyme solutions may work better.

10. If the ground is littered with too much waste, your Mini may seek a cleaner place to eliminate. Scoop the potty area daily, leaving behind just one "reminder."

CHAPTER
6

VET VISITS AND

Your selection of a veterinarian for your dog should be based on personal recommendations of the doctor's skills, and, if possible, his experience with Miniature Schnauzers. If the veterinarian is based nearby, it will be helpful and more convenient because you might have an emergency or need to make multiple visits for treatments.

FIRST STEP: SELECT THE RIGHT VET

All licensed veterinarians are capable of dealing with routine medical issues such as infections and injuries, as well as the promotion of good health (like vaccinations). If the problem affecting your schnauzer is more complex, your vet may refer you to someone with more detailed knowledge of what is wrong. This usually will be a specialist such as a veterinary dermatologist or veterinary ophthalmologist.

Veterinary procedures are very costly and, as treatments improve, they are going to become more expensive. It is quite acceptable to discuss matters of cost with your vet; if there is more than one treatment option, cost may be a factor in deciding which route to take.

Smart owners will look for a vet before they actually need one. For newbie pet owners, start looking for a veterinarian a month or two before you bring home your new Miniature Schnauzer puppy. That will give you time to meet candidate veterinarians, check out the condition of the clinic, meet the staff and see who you feel most comfortable with. If you already have a schnauzer puppy, look sooner rather than later, preferably not in the midst of a veterinary health crisis.

Second, list the qualities that are important to you. Points to consider or investigate:

Convenience: Proximity to your home, extended hours or drop-off services are helpful for people who work regular business hours, have a busy schedule or don't want to drive far. If you have mobility issues, finding a vet who makes house calls or a service that provides pet transport might be particularly important.

Size: A one-person practice will ensure that you will always be dealing with the same vet during each and every visit. "That person can really get to know you and your dog," says Bernadine Cruz, D.V.M., of Laguna Hills Animal Hospital in Laguna Hills, Calif. The downside is that the sole practitioner does not have the immediate input of another vet, and if your vet becomes ill or takes time off, you are out of luck.

A multiple-doctor practice offers consistency if your dog needs to come in unexpectedly on a day when your veterinarian isn't there. Additionally, your vet can quickly consult with his colleagues within the clinic if he's unsure about a diagnosis or a treatment.

If you find a veterinarian within that practice who you really like, you can make your appointments with that individual, establishing the same kind of bond that you would with the solo practitioner.

Appointment Policies: Some practices are by-appointment only, which could minimize your wait time. However, if a sudden problem arises with your Miniature Schnauzer and the veterinarians are booked up, they might not be able to squeeze your pet in that day. Some clinics are walk-in only, which is great for impromptu or crisis visits, but without scheduling may involve longer waits to see the next available veterinarian. Some practices offer the best of both worlds by maintaining an appointment schedule but by also keeping slots open throughout the day for walk-ins.

Basic vs. Full Service vs. State-of-the-Art: A veterinarian practice with high-tech equipment offers greater diagnostic capabilities and treatment options, important for tricky or difficult cases. However, the cost of pricey equipment is passed along to the client, so you could pay more for routine procedures — the bulk of most pets' appointments. Some practices offer boarding, grooming, training classes and other services on the premises — conveniences some pet owners appreciate.

Fees and Payment Polices: How much is a routine visit? If there is a significant price difference, ask why. If you intend to carry health insurance on your Miniature Schnauzer or want to pay by credit card, check that the clinic accepts those payment options.

FIRST VET VISIT

It is much easier, less costly and more effective to practice preventive medicine than

to fight bouts of illness and disease. Properly bred puppies of all breeds come from parents who were selected based upon their genetic disease profile. The puppies' mother should have been vaccinated, free of all internal and external parasites and properly nourished. For these reasons, a visit to the veterinarian who cared for the mother is recommended if at all possible. The mother passes disease resistance to her puppies, which should last from 8 to 10 weeks. Unfortunately, she can also pass on parasites and infection. This is why knowing about her health is useful in learning more about the health of her puppies.

Now that you have your Miniature Schnauzer puppy home safe and sound, it's time to arrange your pup's first trip to the veterinarian. Perhaps the breeder can recommend someone in the area who specializes in Miniature Schnauzers, or maybe you know other Miniature Schnauzer owners who can suggest a good vet. Either way, you should make an appointment within a couple of days of bringing home your puppy. If possible, see if you can stop for this first vet appointment before going home.

The pup's first vet visit will consist of an overall examination to make sure that your pup does not have any problems that are not apparent to you. The veterinarian also will set up a schedule for the pup's vaccinations; the breeder should inform you of which ones your puppy has already received, and the vet can continue from there.

Your puppy also will have his teeth examined and have his skeletal conformation and general health checked prior to certification by the veterinarian. Puppies in certain breeds have problems with their kneecaps, cataracts and other eye problems, heart murmurs and undescended testicles. They may also have behavioral problems, which your veterinarian can evaluate if he or she has had relevant training.

VACCINATION SCHEDULING

Most vaccinations are given by injection and should only be given by a veterinarian. Both you and the vet should keep a record of the date of the injection, the identification of the vaccine and the amount given. Some vets give a first vaccination at 8 weeks of age, but most dog breeders prefer the course not to commence until about 10 weeks

Set up a vet visit before you even bring your new dog home, so you can interview the veterinary staff.

Check with your vet about booster immunizations for your growing Miniature Schnauzer puppy.

In areas with low risk for heartworm disease and fleas, you don't need to give all these chemical preventives: Loading the animal's body up with chemicals on a regular basis increases the risk of adverse immunologic or toxic reactions in susceptible dogs. Feed them healthy diets that don't contain chemical preservatives or other kinds of chemicals. Keep animals away from chemically treated bushes and grass as they can absorb these chemicals through their noses and paws.

— W. Jean Dodds, D.V.M., and president of Hemopet, a nonprofit animal blood bank in Garden Grove, Calif.

because of interaction with the antibodies produced by the mother. The vaccination scheduling is usually based on a 15-day cycle. You must take your vet's advice as to when to vaccinate, as this may differ according to the vaccine used.

The usual vaccines contain immunizing doses of several different viruses such as distemper, parvovirus, parainfluenza and hepatitis. There are other vaccines available when the puppy is at a greater risk of viral exposures. You should rely on your vet's advice. This is especially true for the booster immunizations. Most vaccination programs require a booster when the puppy is a year old and once a year thereafter. In some cases, circumstances may require more frequent immunizations.

Kennel cough, more formally known as *tracheobronchitis*, is combatted with a vaccine that is sprayed into the dog's nostrils. Kennel cough is usually included in routine vaccinations, but it is often not as effective as the vaccines for other major diseases.

Your vet probably will recommend that your Mini puppy be fully vaccinated before you take him on outings. There are airborne diseases, parasite eggs in the grass and unexpected visits from other dogs that might be dangerous to your puppy's health. Other dogs are the most harmful reservoir of pathogenic organisms, as everything they have can be transmitted to your puppy.

6 Months to 1 Year of Age: Unless you intend to breed or show your dog, neutering or spaying your Miniature Schnauzer at 6 months of age is recommended. Discuss this with your veterinarian. Neutering and spaying have proven to be beneficial to male and female puppies, respectively. Besides eliminating the possibility of pregnancy, it inhibits (but does not prevent) breast cancer in females and prostate cancer in male dogs.

Your veterinarian should provide your Miniature Schnauzer puppy with a thorough dental evaluation at 6 months of age, ascertaining whether all his permanent teeth have erupted properly. A home dental care regimen should be initiated by 6 months of age, including weekly brushing and providing good dental devices (such as nylon bones). Regular dental care promotes healthy teeth, fresh breath and a longer life.

Dogs Older Than 1 Year: Proper dietary changes recommended by your veterinarian can make life more pleasant for your aging Miniature Schnauzer and you. Continue to visit the veterinarian at least once a year as bodily functions do change with age. The eyes and ears are no longer as efficient; liver, kidney and intestinal functions often decline.

EVERYDAY HAPPENINGS

Keeping your schnauzer healthy is a matter of keen observation and quick action when necessary. Knowing what's normal for your dog will help you recognize signs of trouble before they blossom into a full-blown emergency situation.

Smart owners won't pick just any vet out of the phone book; they will invest time in researching and interviewing the best vet for their dog.

Raw fruits and vegetables are obviously low in fat. You can buy a bag of baby carrots and flip your dog 10 to 15 baby carrots a day. He'll be fine. If you were to flip him 10 to 15 dog bones a day, your dog wouldn't be able to walk in a year. He'd be a blimp!

— *George Pinkham, D.V.M., of New Milford, N.Y.*

When selecting a vet for your dog, make sure he or she is familiar with Miniature Schnauzers.

Minis Rock

We Love Schnauzers

Even if the problem is minor, such as a cut or scrape, you'll want to care for it immediately to prevent infection, as well as to ensure that your dog doesn't make it worse by chewing or scratching at it. Here's what to do for common, minor injuries or illnesses, and how to recognize and deal with emergencies.

Cuts and Scrapes: For a cut or scrape that's half an inch or smaller, clean the wound with saline solution or warm water and use tweezers to remove any splinters or other debris. Apply an antibiotic ointment. No bandage is necessary unless the wound is on a paw, which can pick up dirt when your dog walks on it. Deep cuts with lots of bleeding or those caused by glass or some other object should be treated by your veterinarian.

Cold Symptoms: Dogs don't actually get colds, but they can get illnesses that have similar symptoms, such as coughing, a runny nose or sneezing. Dogs cough for any number of reasons, from respiratory infections to inhaled irritants to congestive heart failure. Take your Miniature Schnauzer to the veterinarian for prolonged coughing, or coughing accompanied by labored breathing, runny eyes and nose or bloody phlegm.

A runny nose that continues for more than several hours requires veterinary

Stay on top of your dog's health by keeping a record of his vaccinations.

Just like with infants, puppies need a series of vaccinations to ensure that they stay healthy during their first year of life. Download a vaccination chart from **DogChannel.com/Club-Schnauzer** that you can fill out for your Miniature Schnauzer.

attention, as well. If your Miniature Schnauzer sneezes, he may have some mild nasal irritation that will resolve on its own, but frequent sneezing, especially if it's accompanied by a runny nose, may indicate anything from allergies to an infection or something stuck in his nose.

Vomiting and Diarrhea: Sometimes dogs can suffer minor gastric upset when they eat a new type of food, eat too much, eat the contents of the trash can or become excited or anxious. Give your Miniature Schnauzer's stomach a rest by withholding food for 12 hours, and then feeding him a bland diet such as baby food or rice and chicken, gradually returning your dog to his normal food. Projectile vomiting or vomiting or diarrhea that continues for more than 48 hours, is another matter. If this happens, immediately take your Miniature Schnauzer to the veterinarian.

Clogged Anal Glands: A Miniature Schnauzer's anal glands can cause problems if not periodically evacuated. In the wild, dogs regularly clear their anal glands to mark their territory. In domestic dogs, this function is no longer necessary; thus, their contents can build up and clog, caus-

ing discomfort. Signs that the anal glands — located on both sides of the anus — need emptying are if a Miniature Schnauzer drags his rear end along the ground or keeps turning around to lick the area of discomfort.

While care must be taken not to cause injury, anal glands can be evacuated by pressing gently on either side of the anal opening and by using a piece of cotton or a tissue to collect the foul-smelling matter. If anal glands are allowed to become impacted, abscesses can form, causing pain and the need for veterinary attention.

Ingesting Poison: Miniature Schnauzers can get into all sorts of mischief, so it is not uncommon for them to swallow something poisonous in the course of their investigations. Obviously, an urgent visit to the vet is required under such circumstances, but if possible, when you call your vet, inform him which poisonous substance has been ingested, because different treatments are needed. Should it be necessary to cause your schnauzer to vomit (which is not always the case with poisoning), a small lump of baking soda, given orally, will have an immediate effect. Alternatively, a small teaspoon of salt or mustard, dissolved in water, will have a similar effect but may be more difficult to administer and take longer to work.

Teething Tips: Miniature Schnauzer puppies often have painful fits while they are teething. These are not usually serious and are brief. Of course, you must be certain that the cause is nothing more than teething. Giving a puppy something hard to chew on usually will solve this temporary problem.

CHAPTER 7

ON THE TOPIC

OF HEALTH

Healthy, hearty, rugged and resilient are Miniature Schnauzers as an overall breed. Nevertheless, Miniature Schnauzers do carry some defective genes predisposing them to specific genetic diseases: This is neither unusual nor unique to schnauzers or purebred breeds. All mammals — including mixed breed dogs and cats, and even human beings — carry defective genes that can cause genetic disorders; that's just the nature of biology.

Fortunately, Miniature Schnauzer breeders aren't helpless when it comes to dealing with genetic problems: They actively support veterinary research that has or will lead to the screening tools that will empower them to breed away from a hereditary disease. In addition, by studying the family health history of Miniature Schnauzer breeding prospects, conscientious breeders can decide which dogs have the least risk of producing a puppy that will develop diseases such as Cushing's disease, diabetes, epileptic seizures, urinary stones and other problems.

CUSHING'S DISEASE

A common endocrine disorder occurring primarily in middle-aged and older dogs,

Did You Know?

Dogs can get many diseases from ticks, including Lyme disease, Rocky Mountain spotted fever, tick bite paralysis and many others.

Cushing's disease and Cushing's syndrome occur when the adrenal glands secrete excess cortisol. Too much cortisol can contribute to diabetes, urinary tract and skin infections, and high blood pressure, which, in turn, can lead to cardiovascular or cardiopulmonary effects.

In about 85 percent of cases, cortisol overproduction is caused by a tumor in the pituitary gland, which stimulates the adrenal glands. The remaining cases are caused by an adrenal tumor that secretes too much cortisol on its own. Cushing's disease specifically refers to the pituitary-dependent form; Cushing's syndrome refers to either. Pituitary tumors are nearly always benign, whereas adrenal tumors can be benign or malignant.

Signs of Cushing's disease can include excessive thirst and urination, a ravenous appetite, panting and bilateral symmetrical hair loss along the trunk and sometimes the tail. The dog can also have a pot-bellied appearance, muscle weakness, obesity or recurrent infections due to the immunosuppression caused by excess cortisol. Because clinical signs are not specific to Cushing's, a chemistry panel, a complete blood count and a urinalysis should be performed to rule out diseases that can mimic Cushing's and to look for the typical Cushing's markers (i.e., increased alkaline phosphatase). From there, a more definitive diagnosis can be obtained through specific endocrine blood tests.

Preferred treatment for adrenal-based Cushing's is surgical removal of the affected adrenal gland. If surgery is not an option for medical, financial or other reasons, lifelong drug therapy — lysodren, ketoconazole or trilostane — can be used.

DIABETES

Diabetes occurs when a dog is unable to adequately produce or properly use insulin (a hormone necessary for regulating glucose, a necessary energy source for sustaining life). Without sufficient insulin, the body breaks down fat and protein stores to use as alternative energy sources, and glucose levels rise in the bloodstream. Untreated, dogs can develop complications including cataracts, blindness, infections, pancreatitis (inflammation of the pancreas) or diabetic ketoacidosis, a serious metabolic condition from which the dog could die. The age of diabetes onset is typically middle age (7 to 9 years) and older. Signs include increased thirst and urination, increased appetite, and sometimes weight loss and lethargy.

A combination of the dog's history, physical exam findings and laboratory analysis checks for either high sugar levels in the blood or urine. The diagnosis is made by confirming persistent, ideally fasted, hyperglycemia to rule out the possibility of high blood sugar secondary to diet, other hormones or stress.

Diabetes is managed through insulin injections, weight management, dietary control and regular monitoring. Nearly all diabetic dogs have Type I diabetes, meaning they need insulin and cannot be managed with diet or oral medications that are frequently used in people.

Generally, insulin shots must be administered (usually by a dog's owner) twice daily, in 12-hour intervals, in order to maintain consistent insulin levels. Because different dogs respond better to one type of insulin over another, and to different dosage amounts, the vet will initially have to monitor and re-evaluate the dog every few days to see how the dog is responding and make adjustments accordingly. This evaluation may be as simple as a phone conversation.

Diet regimen should consist of a high fiber diet with complex carbohydrates, feed-

Dogs wear head cones after surgery to restrict their head movement so they can't lick or bite wounds or stitches.

ing set amounts at the same time and avoiding leftovers and treats (which could spike sugar levels). Weight control is also important, as obesity can cause insulin resistance.

Effective management also relies on observation and monitoring. Dog owners should become treatment partners with their veterinarians by measuring daily water intake, checking urine sugars and noting the dog's appetite. Urine sugar monitoring can easily be performed at home by collecting morning urine sample then utilizing urine dips sticks available at most pharmacies. Dogs should be re-evaluated by the veterinarian initially monthly, then every three months once reasonable control is established, not only to check their glucose levels but also to make sure they're not developing urinary tract infections problems, a common complication in diabetic dogs.

With proper diet and adherence to drug therapy, prognosis is quite good. Life expectancy may be somewhat shorter because these dogs are prone to infection, pancreatitis, etc., but otherwise most well-managed dogs lead normal lives.

EPILEPSY

Idiopathic epilepsy is a disorder associated with recurrent seizures that are not a consequence of other disorders, such as head trauma, low blood sugar, poisoning, heart disease, kidney or liver failure, or electrolyte imbalances. Seen in dozens of dog breeds, idiopathic epilepsy is one of the most common diseases of the nervous system in dogs. However, it's difficult to diagnose because seizures can occur for several reasons, and there is no actual epilepsy test. Hence, the diagnosis is actually made by eliminating other possible causes — a diagnosis of exclusion.

"The onset of idiopathic epilepsy generally occurs between the ages of 1 and 5 years," says Steven Zinderman, D.V.M., medical director at Roadside Veterinary Clinic in Highland, Mich. Typical seizures, called tonic-clonic grand mal seizures, cause a dog to stiffen, vocalize, lose control of his bowel and urinary function or drool excessively. This tonic phase could last up to 30 seconds.

"The clonic phase follows, during which your dog may paddle his legs as if he were running, experience facial and muscle twitching and chomp his jaws; this could last 60 seconds," Zinderman says. "During the whole process, your dog is unconscious and could have irregular breathing. Breathing returns to normal once the seizure ends."

To obtain a diagnosis, your veterinarian will run several tests — blood-work, urinalysis, toxin scan, liver and thyroid function — to pinpoint or rule out other causes. Your veterinarian also may refer your dog to a veterinary neurologist for Magnetic Resonance Imaging (commonly called MRI) or a Computerized Tomography (or CT) scan of the brain, an analysis of spinal fluid and an electroencephalogram.

Although there is no cure for idiopathic epilepsy, in most cases the disease can be managed. "The most common drugs used to treat epilepsy are the anti-seizure drugs phenobarbital and potassium bromide," Zinderman says. "These are sometimes used in combination and must be adjusted for each patient. Some medications may make your pet drowsy, but this should not restrict his activity. But not all patients are treated with medication. If your dog's seizures are mild and don't occur more than once every few months, treatment may not be necessary."

URINARY STONES

Urinary crystals and stones occur when minerals that normally dissolve during the production of urine fail to dissolve. As a result, these stones can irritate the bladder lining, increasing the risk of developing a urinary tract infection, and, if they become large enough, partially or completely obstruct urine flow. If total obstruction remains unrelieved, urine backs up into the system instead of being expelled, and the animal can die within 48 to 72 hours. Although stones and crystals can form anywhere in the urinary tract, they are usually found in the bladder.

Small breed dogs along with a few other larger breeds have increased incidence of stones. The most common types of stones seen in the Miniature Schnauzer are struvite (composed of magnesium ammonium

SMART TIP!

Many canine skin irritations can be reduced or simply avoided by employing a simple preventive regimen:

- Keep your schnauzer's skin clean and dry.
- Shampoo your dog regularly (especially during allergy season) with a hypoallergenic shampoo.
- Rinse the coat thoroughly.
- Practice good flea control.
- Supplement your dog's diet with fatty acids, such as omega-3.

phosphate, commonly associated with urinary tract infections and an alkaline pH) and calcium oxalate (associated with elevated calcium levels in the blood and an acid pH). Signs include blood the in urine, straining to urinate with/without urine passing, discomfort and inappropriate urination (accidents).

Most struvite stones are treated with special diets and concurrent antibiotics. These diets are designed to create a dilute urine (which helps flush out crystals), an acidic urine pH (a more soluble environment for struvite stones) and lower levels of magnesium and phosphorus (which contribute to the formation of struvite).

During diet dissolution, the pet should only be fed the dissolution diet, because any supplementation or treats may cause the urine to be less than ideal. Your veterinarian will frequently monitor the dog with X-rays to determine the presence and size of the dissolving stones and watch for signs of urinary tract obstruction (straining to urinate, passing blood, feeling ill) as small stones that are dissolving may lodge in the urinary tract.

Any stone removed surgically or passed in the urine should be analyzed to determine its chemical composition so the appropriate regiment for treatment and prevention can be instituted.

Some types of stones are recurrent and may require more aggressive monitoring.

Both types can reoccur if the urine is not monitored carefully and preventative diets and other medications not consistently given.

OTHER HEALTH CONCERNS

Airborne allergies: Just as humans suffer from hay fever during allergy season, many dogs suffer from the same. When the pollen count is high, your Mini might suffer, but don't expect him to sneeze or have a runny nose like a human. Schnauzers react to pollen allergies in the same way they react to fleas; they scratch and bite themselves. Dogs, like humans, can be tested for allergens. Be sure to discuss allergy testing with your vet.

Summertime allergies can affect your schnauzer, too!

Autoimmune illness: An autoimmune illness is one in which the immune system overacts and does not recognize parts of the affected person. Instead, the immune system starts to react as if these parts were foreign cells and need to be destroyed. An example of an autoimmune illness is rheumatoid arthritis, which occurs when the body does not recognize the joints. This leads to a very painful and damaging reaction in the joints. Rheumatoid arthritis has nothing to do with age, so it can also occur in puppies. The wear-and-tear arthritis in older people or dogs is called osteoarthritis.

Lupus is another autoimmune disease that affects dogs as well as people. It can take variable forms, affecting the kidneys, bones and skin. It can be fatal, so it is treated with steroids, which have very significant side effects. Steroids calm down the allergic reaction to the body's tissues, which helps the lupus, but also affects the body's reaction to actual foreign cells such as bacteria; it also thins the skin and bones.

Food Allergies and Intolerance: Properly feeding your Schnauzer is very important. An incorrect diet could affect your dog's health, behavior and nervous system, possibly making a normal dog aggressive. The result of a good or bad diet is most visible in a dog's skin and coat, but internal organs are affected, too.

Dogs are allergic to many foods that are popular and even recommended by breeders and veterinarians. Changing the brand of food may not eliminate the problem if the ingredient to which your dog is allergic is contained in the new brand.

Recognizing a food allergy can be difficult. Humans often have rashes or swelling of the lips or eyes when they eat foods they are allergic to. Dogs do not usually develop rashes, but they react the same way they do

to an airborne allergy or parasite bite; they itch, scratch and bite. While pollen allergies and parasite bites are usually seasonal, food allergies are year-round problems.

Diagnosis of a food allergy is based on a two- to four-week dietary trial with a home-cooked diet, excluding all other foods. The diet should consist of boiled rice or potato with a source of protein that your Mini has never eaten before, such as fresh or frozen fish, lamb or even something as exotic as pheasant. Water has to be the only drink, and it is important that no other foods are fed during this trial. If your dog's condition improves, try the original diet again to see if the itching resumes. If it does, then your dog is allergic to his original diet. You must find a diet that does not distress your dog's skin. Start with a commercially available hypoallergenic food or the homemade diet that you created for the allergy trial.

Food intolerance is the inability to completely digest certain foods. This occurs because the dog does not have the enzymes necessary to digest some foodstuffs. All puppies have the enzymes needed to digest canine milk, but some dogs do not have the enzymes to digest cow milk, resulting in loose bowels, stomach pains and flatulence.

Dogs often do not have the enzymes to digest soy or other beans. The treatment is to exclude these foods from your Mini's diet.

EXTERNAL PARASITES

Insect bites itch, erupt and can become infected. Dogs have the same reaction to fleas, ticks and mites. When an insect lands on you, you can whisk it away. Unfortunately, when your Miniature Schnauzer is bitten by a flea, tick or mite, he can only scratch or bite.

By the time your schnauzer has been bitten, the parasite has done its damage. It may have laid eggs, which will cause further problems. The itching from parasite bites is probably due to the saliva injected into the site when the parasite sucks the dog's blood.

Fleas: Of all the health and grooming problems to which canines are susceptible, none is better known and more frustrating than fleas. Flea infestation is relatively simple to cure but difficult to prevent.

To control flea infestation, you have to understand the flea's lifecycle. Fleas are often thought of as a summertime problem, but centrally heated homes have made fleas a year-round problem. The most effective method of flea control is a two-stage approach: kill the adult fleas, then control the development of pupae (pre-

SMART TIP!

Brush your dog's teeth every day. Plaque colonizes on the tooth surface in as little as six to eight hours, and if not removed by brushing, forms calculus (tartar) within three to five days. Plaque and tartar cause gum disease, periodontal disease, loosening of the teeth and tooth loss. In bad cases of dental disease, bacteria from the mouth can get into the bloodstream, leading to kidney or heart problems — both of which can be life shortening.

adult) fleas. Unfortunately, no single active ingredient is effective against all stages of the flea lifecycle.

Treating fleas should be a two-pronged attack. First, the environment needs to be treated; this includes carpets and furniture, especially your Mini's bedding and areas underneath furniture. The environment should be treated with a household spray containing an insect growth regulator and an insecticide to kill the adult fleas. Most insecticides are effective against eggs and larvae; they actually mimic the fleas' own hormones and stop the eggs and larvae from developing into adult fleas. There are currently no treatments available to attack the pupae stage of the lifecycle, so the adult insecticide is used to kill the newly hatched adult fleas before they find a host. Most insect growth regulators are active for many months, while adult insecticides are only active for a few days.

When treating fleas with a household spray, vacuum before applying the product. This stimulates as many pupae as possible to hatch into adult fleas. The vacuum cleaner should also be treated with an insecticide to prevent the eggs and larvae that have been collected in the vacuum bag from hatching.

The second stage of treatment is to apply an adult insecticide to your Miniature Schnauzer. Traditionally, this would be in the form of a collar or a spray. Recent innovations include digestible insecticides that poison the fleas when they ingest the dog's blood. Alternatively, there are drops that, when placed on the back of the dog's neck, spread throughout the hair and skin to kill adult fleas.

Ticks: Though not as common as fleas, ticks are found all over the tropical and temperate world. They don't bite like fleas; they harpoon. They dig their sharp *proboscis* (nose) into the Mini's skin and drink the blood, which is their only food and drink. Ticks are controlled the same way fleas are controlled.

The American dog tick, *Dermacentor variabilis,* may be the most common dog tick in many areas, especially those areas where the climate is hot and humid. Most dog ticks have life expectancies of a week to 6 months, depending on climatic conditions. They can neither jump nor fly, but they can crawl slowly and can travel up to 16 feet to reach a sleeping or unsuspecting dog.

Mites: Just as fleas and ticks can be problematic for your dog, mites can also lead to an itch fit. Microscopic in size, mites are related to ticks and generally take up permanent residence on their host animal — in this case, a Mini. The term "mange" refers to any infestation caused by one of the mighty mites, of which there are six varieties that smart dog owners should know about.

■ Demodex mites cause a condition known as *demodicosis* (sometimes called "red mange" or "follicular mange"), in which the mites live in the dog's hair follicles and sebaceous glands in larger-than-normal numbers. Most dogs recover from this type of mange without any treatment, though topical therapies are commonly prescribed by a veterinarian.

■ The *Cheyletiellosis* mite is the hook-mouthed culprit associated with "walking dandruff," a condition that affects dogs as well as cats and rabbits. If untreated, this mange can affect a whole kennel of dogs and can be spread to humans as well.

■ The *Sarcoptes* mite causes intense itching on the dog in the form of a condition known as scabies or sarcoptic mange. Scabies is highly contagious and can be passed to humans. Sometimes an allergic reaction to the mite worsens the severe itching associated with sarcoptic mange.

■ Ear mites, *Otodectes cynotis,* lead to otodectic mange, which commonly affects the outer ear canal of the dog, though other areas can be affected as well. Your vet can prescribe a treatment to flush out the ears and kill any eggs. A complete month of treatment is necessary to cure this mange.

■ Two other mites, less common in dogs, include *Dermanyssus gallinae* (the "poultry" or "red" mite) and *Eutrombicula alfreddugesi* (the North American mite associated with *trombiculidiasis* or chigger infestation). The types of mange caused by both of these mites must be treated by vets.

INTERNAL PARASITES

Most animals — fish, birds and mammals, including dogs and humans — have worms and other parasites that live inside their bodies. According to Dr. Herbert R. Axelrod, a fish pathologist, there are two kinds of parasites: "smart" and "dumb." The smart parasites live in peaceful cooperation with their hosts — a symbiotic relationship — while the dumb parasites kill their hosts.

Most worm infections are relatively easy to control. If they are not controlled, they weaken the host dog to the point that other medical problems occur, but they do not kill the host as dumb parasites would.

Roundworms: They live in the dog's intestines and continually shed eggs. It has been estimated that a dog produces more than six ounces of feces every day; each ounce averages hundreds of thousands of roundworm eggs. There are no known areas in which dogs roam that do not contain roundworm eggs. Roundworms infect people, too, so have your dog regularly tested.

An ounce of prevention is worth a pound of cure in the case of parasites.

Roundworm infection can kill puppies and cause severe problems in adult dogs, as the hatched larvae travel to the lungs and trachea through the bloodstream. Cleanliness is the best prevention against roundworms. Always pick up after your dog and dispose of feces in appropriate receptacles.

Hookworms: Hookworms are dangerous to humans as well as to dogs and cats, and can cause of severe iron-deficiency anemia. The worm uses its teeth to attach itself to the dog's intestines and changes the site of its attachment about six times per day. Each time the worm repositions itself, the dog loses blood and can become anemic. Symptoms of hookworm infection include dark stools, weight loss, general weakness, pale coloration and anemia, as well as possible skin problems. Fortunately, hookworms are easily purged with a number of medications that have proven effective. Discuss these with your veterinarian. Most heartworm preventives include a hookworm insecticide.

Humans can be infected by hookworms through exposure to contaminated feces. Because the worms cannot complete their lifecycle in a human, the worms simply infest the skin and cause irritation. As a preventive, use disposable gloves or a poop scoop to pick up your schnauzer's droppings and prevent your dog (or neighborhood cats) from defecating in children's play areas.

Tapeworms: There are many species of tapeworms, all of which are carried by fleas. Fleas are so small that your Mini could pass them onto your hands, your plate or your food, making it possible for you to ingest a flea that is carrying tapeworm eggs. While a tapeworm infection is not life threatening in dogs (it's a *smart* parasite!),

if transmitted to humans, it can be the cause of a serious liver disease.

Whipworms: In North America, whipworms are counted among the most common parasitic worms in dogs. Affected dogs may only experience upset tummies, colic and diarrhea. These worms, however, can live for months or years in the dog, beginning their larval stage in the small intestine, spending their adult life in the large intestine and finally passing infective eggs through the dog's feces. The only way to detect whipworms is through a fecal examination, though this is not always foolproof. Treatment for whipworms is tricky, due to the worms' unusual lifecycle, and often dogs are reinfected due to exposure to infective eggs on the ground. Cleaning up droppings in your backyard and in public places is necessary for sanitary purposes and the health of your dog and others.

Threadworms: Though less common than roundworms and hookworms, threadworms concern dog owners in the southwestern United States and the Gulf Coast area where the climate is hot and humid, which is the prime environment for threadworms. Living in the small intestine of the dog, this worm measures a mere two millimeters and is round in shape. Like the whipworm, the threadworm's lifecycle is very complex and the eggs and larvae are transported through the feces.

A deadly disease in humans, threadworms readily infect people, mostly through the handling of feces. Threadworms are most often seen in young puppies. The most common symptoms include bloody diarrhea and pneumonia. Infected puppies must be promptly isolated and treated to prevent spreading the threadworms to other dogs and humans; vets recommend a follow-up treatment one month later.

Heartworms: These thin, extended worms measure up to 12 inches long and live in a dog's heart and inhabit the major blood vessels around it. Dogs may have up to 200 heartworms. Symptoms may be loss of energy, loss of appetite, coughing, the development of a pot belly and anemia.

Heartworms are transmitted by mosquitoes, which drink the blood of infected dogs and take in larvae with the blood. The larvae, called *microfilariae*, develop within the body of the mosquito and are then passed on to the next dog bitten after the larvae mature.

It takes two to three weeks for the larvae to develop to the infective stage within the body of the mosquito. Dogs are usually treated at about 6 weeks of age and are maintained on a prophylactic dose given monthly to regulate proliferation.

Although this is a dangerous disease, it is difficult for a dog to be infected. Discuss the various preventives with your veterinarian, because there are many different types now available. Together, you can decide on a safe course of prevention for your Miniature Schnauzer.

Regularly scheduled grooming sessions keep a schnauzer looking good, as well as keeping him healthier.

Y ou have probably heard it a thousand times: You are what you eat. Believe it or not, it is very true. For Miniature Schnauzers, they are what you feed them because they have little choice in the matter. Even smart owners who want to feed their Minis the best often cannot do so because it can be so confusing. With the overwhelming assortment of dog foods, it's difficult to figure out which one is truly best for their dogs. Let's shed some light on the confusion.

BASIC TYPES

Dog foods are produced in various types: dry, wet, semimoist and frozen.

Dry food is useful for cost-conscious owners because it tends to be less expensive than the others. These foods also contain the least fat and the most preservatives. Dry food is bulky and takes longer to eat than other foods, so it's more filling.

Wet food — available in cans or foil pouches — is usually 60 to 70 percent water and is more expensive than dry. A palatable source of concentrated nutrition, wet food also makes a good supplement for underweight dogs or those recovering from illness.

it's a Fact

Bones can cause gastrointestinal obstruction and perforation, and may be contaminated with salmonella or E. coli. Leave them in the trash and give your dog a nylon toy bone instead.

Some smart owners add a little wet food to dry to increase its appeal.

Semimoist food is flavorful, but it usually contains lots of sugar. That can lead to dental problems and obesity. Therefore, semimoist food is not a good choice for your Miniature Schnauzer's main diet.

Likewise, **frozen food**, which is available in cooked and in raw forms, is usually more expensive than wet foods. The advantages of frozen food are similar to those of wet foods.

The amount of food that your Miniature Schnauzer needs depends on a number of factors, such as his age, activity level, the quality of the food, reproductive status (if your schnauzer is a female) and size. What's the easiest way to figure it out? Start with the manufacturer's recommended amount, then adjust it according to your dog's response. For example, feed the recommended amount for a few weeks, and if your schnauzer loses weight, increase the amount by 10 to 20 percent. If your Miniature Schnauzer gains weight, decrease the amount. It won't take long to determine the amount of food that keeps your best friend in optimal condition.

NUTRITION 101

All schnauzers (and all dogs, for that matter) need proteins, carbohydrates, fats, vitamins and minerals to be in peak condition.

■ **Proteins** are used for growth and repair of muscles, bones and other tissues. They're also used for the production of antibodies, enzymes and hormones. All dogs need protein, but it's especially important for puppies because they grow and develop so quickly. Protein sources include various types of meat, meat meal, meat byproducts, eggs and dairy products.

■ **Carbohydrates** are metabolized into glucose, the body's principal energy source. Carbohydrates are available as sugars, starches and fiber.

• Sugars (simple carbohydrates) are not suitable nutrient sources for dogs.

• Starches — a preferred carbohydrate in dog food — are found in a variety of plant

Semimoist food has lots of sugar in it.

Your Miniature Schnauzer can't read the labels, so he looks to you to provide the best possible nutrition that you can afford.

Believe it or not, during your schnauzer's lifetime, you'll buy a few thousand pounds of dog food! Go to **DogChannel.com/ Club-Schnauzer** and download a chart that outlines the average cost of dog food.

products. Starches must be cooked in order to be digested.

- Fiber (cellulose) — also a preferred type of carbohydrate found in dog food — isn't digestible but helps the digestive tract function properly.

■ **Fats** are also a source of energy and play an important role in maintaining your schnauzer's skin and coat health, hormone production, nervous system function and vitamin transport. However, you must be aware of the fact that fats increase the palatability and the calorie count of dog food, which can lead to serious health problems, such as obesity, for puppies or dogs who are allowed to overindulge. Some foods contain added amounts of omega fatty acids such as docosohexaenoic acid, a compound that may enhance brain development and learning in puppies but is not considered an essential nutrient by the Association of American Feed Control Officials (www.aafco.org). Fats used in dog foods include tallow, lard, poultry fat, fish oil and vegetable oils.

■ **Vitamins** and **minerals** are essential to dogs for proper muscle and nerve function, bone growth, healing, metabolism and fluid balance. Especially important for your schnauzer puppy are calcium, phosphorus and vitamin D, which must be supplied in the right balance to ensure proper development and maintenance of bones and teeth.

Did You Know?

Because semimoist food contains lots of sugar, it isn't a good selection for your schnauzer's main menu. However, it is great for an occasional yummy snack. Try forming into little balls for a once-a-week treat! She'll love ya for it!

Dogs of all ages love treats and table food, but these goodies can unbalance your Miniature Schnauzer's diet and lead to a weight problem if you don't feed him wisely. Table food, whether fed as a treat or as part of a meal, shouldn't account for more than 10 percent of your dog's daily caloric intake. If you plan to give your Miniature Schnauzer treats, be sure to include "treat calories" when calculating your daily food requirement — so you don't end up with a pudgy pup!

When shopping for packaged treats, look for ones that provide complete nutrition. They're basically dog food in a fun form. Choose crunchy goodies for chewing fun and dental health. Other ideas for tasty treats include:

✓ small chunks of cooked, lean meat
✓ dry dog food morsels
✓ cheese
✓ veggies (cooked, raw or frozen)
✓ breads, crackers or dry cereal
✓ unsalted, unbuttered, plain, popped popcorn

Some foods, however, can be dangerous or even deadly to a dog. The following can cause digestive upset (vomiting or diarrhea) or fatal toxic reactions:

✗ **avocados:** if eaten in sufficient quantity these can cause gastrointestinal irritation, with vomiting and diarrhea

✗ **baby food:** may contain onion powder; does not provide balanced nutrition

✗ **chocolate:** contains methylxanthines and theobromine, caffeine-like compounds that can cause vomiting, diarrhea, heart abnormalities, tremors, seizures and death. Darker chocolates contain higher levels of the toxic compounds.

✗ **eggs, raw:** whites contain an enzyme that prevents uptake of biotin, a B vitamin; may contain salmonella

✗ **garlic (and related foods):** can cause gastrointestinal irritation and anemia if eaten in sufficient quantity

✗ **grapes:** can cause kidney failure if eaten in sufficient quantity (the toxic dose varies from dog to dog)

✗ **macadamia nuts:** can cause vomiting, weakness, lack of coordination and other problems

✗ **meat, raw:** may contain harmful bacteria such as salmonella or E. coli

✗ **milk:** can cause diarrhea in some puppies

✗ **onions (and related foods):** can cause gastrointestinal irritation and anemia if eaten in sufficient quantity

✗ **raisins:** can cause kidney failure if eaten in sufficient quantity (the toxic dose varies from dog to dog)

✗ **yeast bread dough:** can rise in the gastrointestinal tract, causing obstruction; produces alcohol as it rises

Just as your Miniature Schnauzer receives proper nutrition from his food, water is an essential nutrient, as well. Water keeps your dog's body hydrated and facilitates normal function of the body's systems. During housetraining, it is necessary to keep an eye on how much water your Miniature Schnauzer is drinking, but once he is reliably trained, he should have access to clean, fresh water at all times, especially if you feed him dry food. Make sure that your dog's water bowl is clean, and change the water often.

CHECK OUT THE LABEL

To help you get a feel for what you are feeding your dog, start by taking a look at the label on the package or can. Look for the words "complete and balanced." This tells you that the food meets specific nutritional requirements set by the AAFCO for either adults ("maintenance") or puppies and pregnant/lactating females ("growth and reproduction"). The label must state the group for which the food is intended. If you're feeding a puppy, choose a "growth and reproduction" food.

The nutrition label also includes a list of minimum protein, minimum fat, maximum fiber and maximum moisture content. (You won't find carbohydrate content because it's everything that isn't protein, fat, fiber and moisture.)

The nutritional analysis refers to crude protein and crude fat — amounts that have been determined in the laboratory. This analysis is technically accurate, but it does not tell you anything about digestibility: how much of the particular nutrient your Miniature Schnauzer can actually use. For information about digestibility, contact the manufacturer (check the label for a telephone number and website address).

Did You Know? If you're feeding a puppy food that's complete and balanced, your young schnauzer doesn't need any dietary supplements such as vitamins, minerals or other types of food. In fact, dietary supplements could even harm your puppy by unbalancing his diet. If you have questions about supplementing your schnauzer's diet, ask your veterinarian.

Virtually all commercial puppy foods exceed AAFCO's minimal requirements for protein and fat, the two nutrients most commonly evaluated when comparing foods. Protein levels in dry puppy foods usually range from about 26 to 30 percent; for canned foods, the values are about 9 to 13 percent. The fat content of dry puppy foods is about 20 percent or more; for canned foods, it's 8 percent or more. (Dry food values are larger than canned food values because dry food contains less water; the values are actually similar when compared on a dry matter basis.)

Finally, check the ingredients on the label, which lists the ingredients in descending order by weight. Manufacturers are allowed to separately list different forms of a single ingredient (e.g., ground corn and corn gluten meal). The food may contain meat byproducts, meat and bone meal, and animal fat, which probably won't appeal to you but are nutritious and safe for your puppy. Higher quality foods usually have meat or meat products near the top of the ingredient list, but you don't need to worry about grain products as long as the label indicates that the food is nutritionally complete. Dogs are omnivores (not carnivores, as commonly believed), so all balanced dog foods contain animal and plant ingredients.

STORE IT RIGHT

Properly storing your Miniature Schnauzer's food will ensure that it maintains its quality, nutrient content and taste. Here's what to do before and after you open that package or can.

◆ Dry food should be stored in a cool, dry bug- and vermin-free place, especially if it's a preservative-free product. Many manufacturers include an expiration date on the package label, but this usually refers to the shelf life of the unopened package. For optimal quality, don't buy more dry food than your Miniature Schnauzer can eat in one month. To store dry food after opening the bag, fold the bag top down several times and secure it with a clip or empty the contents into a food-grade airtight plastic container (available at pet-supply and discount stores). Make sure the storage container is clean and dry and has never been used to store toxic materials.

◆ Canned food, if unopened, can remain good for three years or longer, but it's best to use it within one year of purchase. Discard puffy cans or those that are leaking fluid. Leftover canned food should be covered and refrigerated, then used within three days.

◆ Frozen food can be stored for at least one year in the freezer. Longer storage can cause deterioration of the quality and

Your dog needs access to plenty of fresh, clean water each day.

Feeding your schnauzer is part of your daily routine. Take a break, and have some fun online and play "Feed the Schnauzer," an exclusive game found only on **DogChannel.com/ Club-Schnauzer** — just click on "Games."

taste of the food. Thaw frozen food in the refrigerator or use the defrost setting of your microwave. Cover and refrigerate leftovers, which should be used within 24 hours.

Eating healthy isn't easy — not even for a dog. Limit snacks and between-meal treats.

STAGES OF LIFE

When selecting your dog's diet, three stages of development must be considered: the puppy stage, the adult stage and the senior stage.

Puppy Diets: Pups instinctively want to nurse, and a normal puppy will exhibit this behavior from just a few moments following birth. Puppies should be allowed to nurse for about the first six weeks, although by the third or fourth week, the breeder will begin to introduce small portions of suitable solid food. Most breeders like to initially introduce alternate milk and solid food meals, leading up to weaning time.

By the time Miniature Schnauzer puppies are 7 weeks old (or a maximum of 8), they should be fully weaned and fed solely on puppy food. Selection of the most suitable, high-quality food at this time is essential because a puppy's fastest growth rate is during the first year of life. Seek advice about your dog's diet from your veterinarian. The frequency of meals will be reduced over time, and when a young dog has reached 10 to 12 months, he should be switched to an adult diet.

Puppy and junior diets can be well balanced for the needs of your Miniature Schnauzer so that, except in certain circumstances, additional vitamin, mineral and protein supplements will not be required.

How often should you feed your Miniature Schnauzer in a day? Puppies have small stomachs and high metabolic rates, so they need to eat several times a day to consume sufficient nutrients. If your puppy is younger than 3 months old, feed him four or five meals a day. When your Miniature Schnauzer is 3 to 5 months old, decrease the number of meals to three or four. At 6 months, most puppies can move to an adult schedule of two meals a day.

Adult Diets: A dog is considered an adult when he has stopped growing. Rely on your veterinarian or dietary specialist to recommend an acceptable maintenance diet. Major dog food manufacturers specialize in this type of food, and smart owners must select the one best suited to their dogs'

schnauzer usually exercises less, moves more slowly and sleeps more.

This change in his lifestyle and physiological performance requires a change in diet. Because these changes take place slowly, they might not be recognizable at first. These metabolic changes increase the tendency toward obesity, requiring an even more vigilant approach to feeding. Obesity in an older dog exacerbates the health problems that already accompany old age.

As a Miniature Schnauzer ages, few of his organs function up to par. The kidneys slow down, and the intestines become less efficient. These age-related factors are

needs. Do not leave food out all day for free feeding, as this freedom inevitably translates to inches around the dog's waist.

Senior Diets: As dogs get older, their metabolism begins to change. A senior

SMART TIP!

How can you tell if your Miniature Schnauzer is fit or fat? When you run your hands down your pal's sides from front to back, you should be able to easily feel her ribs. It's OK if you feel a little body fat (and a lot of hair), but you shouldn't feel huge fat pads. You should also be able to feel your schnauzer's waist — an indentation behind the ribs.

best handled with a change in your schnauzer's diet and a change in feeding schedule to give smaller portions that are more easily digested.

There is no single best diet for an older Miniature Schnauzer. While many older dogs will do perfectly fine on light or senior diets, other dogs will do better on special premium diets such as lamb and rice. Be sensitive to your senior Miniature Schnauzer's diet, and this will help control other problems that may arise with your old friend.

A fat Mini is no laughing matter. Keep your dog fit and healthy.

These delicious, dog-friendly recipes will have your furry friend smacking her lips and salivating for more. Just remember: Treats aren't meant to replace your dog's regular meals. Give your schnauzer snacks sparingly and continue to feed her nutritious, well-balanced meals.

Cheddar Squares

$1/3$ cup all-natural applesauce
$1/3$ cup low-fat cheddar cheese, shredded
$1/3$ cup water
2 cups unbleached white flour

In a medium bowl, mix all the wet ingredients. In a large bowl, mix the flour. Slowly add all the wet ingredients to the flour mixture.

Mix well. Pour batter into a greased, 13x9x2-inch pan. Bake at 375-degrees Fahrenheit for 25 to 30 minutes. Bars are done when a toothpick inserted in the center and removed comes out clean. Cool and cut into bars. This recipe makes about 54, $1^{1}/_{2}$-inch bars.

Peanut Butter Bites

3 tablespoons vegetable oil
$1/4$ cup smooth peanut butter, no salt or sugar
$1/4$ cup honey
$1^{1}/_{2}$ teaspoon baking powder
2 eggs
2 cups whole wheat flour

In a large bowl, mix all ingredients until dough is firm. If the dough is too sticky, mix in a small amount of flour. Knead dough on a lightly floured surface until firm. Roll out dough half an inch thick, and cut with cookie cutters. Put cookies on a cookie sheet half an inch apart. Bake at 350-degrees Fahrenheit for 20 to 25 minutes. When done, cookies should be firm to the touch. Turn oven off and leave cookies for one to two hours to harden. This recipe makes about 40, 2-inch-long cookies.

CHAPTER 9

GROOMING

GUIDE

With his robust, squared-away body and the stern expression of that bushy-browed ancestor who scowled down at you from the wall of your grandmother's parlor, the Miniature Schnauzer is a walking contradiction. Beneath that baronial bearing, beats the heart of a silly little clown in a spiffy uniform with a devotion to his family that knows no bounds. As dedicated devotees will attest, owning one of these droll canine characters usually means being hooked for life on this delightful breed.

Before succumbing to the charms of this spunky companion, you should be aware that the Miniature Schnauzer is not a wash-and-wear pet. To stay so handsome, this breed needs a thorough brushing at least twice a week and professional grooming every four to eight weeks, depending on how well you maintain him between salon visits. Although some really eager owners master the skills of grooming their own schnauzer, a professional groomer, who knows and loves the breed, is a smart owner's best bet in maintaining the peerless image of this highly-polished gem of the canine family.

Did You Know?

Nail clipping can be tricky, so many dog owners leave that task for the professionals. However, if you walk your dog on concrete, you may not have to worry about it. The concrete acts like a nail file and will help keep the nails neatly trimmed.

To be properly groomed and maintained, your dog will need to have a cooperative attitude. In turn, you will need to be relaxed and loving as you let your pup know who the top dog is in your family as you assume your new role of surrogate parent. Because most owners acquire their puppy at 8 to 12 weeks of age, instruction in grooming manners is every bit as important as housetraining your pup. It is imperative to get your schnauzer used to handling from an early age before he starts throwing a tantrum every time he sees the brush. Behaviorists call this period in a puppy's development the "fear imprint stage" because experiences that frighten the young-

ster during this time may continue to affect him for the rest of his life. Getting used to your touch helps prevent a fear response to people and a reluctance to the grooming process as well.

SCHNAUZER AT A GLANCE

Schnauzer, translated from the German "*schnauze*," means muzzle or beard, which is undoubtedly the breed's most recognizable characteristic. Long and luxurious, it adds character to the dog's handsome face and also highlights the need for grooming.

To look his best, the Mini Schnauzer's coat should be either hand stripped (a process in which loose hair is removed by hand or with a special tool) or clippered. His furnishings, from his distinctive eyebrows to the flowing fullness of his cylindrical legs, should be trimmed to perfection. Balance is the groomer's goal in enhancing his sharp image.

When a Miniature Schnauzer's outer coat is hand stripped or plucked, the breed's double coat is maintained. Minis shown in conformation are always hand stripped, never clipped, except for the head and private areas. Hand stripping, however, is very time-intensive and requires knowing which areas grow at a fast or slow rate. It is not just a matter of randomly pulling hairs but rather a strategic grooming process designed to shape and show the coat to its best advantage. Those who show schnauzers usually strip their coats over three or four months, beginning with the area they want to be the longest when the dog is shown.

Keep in mind that whatever the season, it's always easy for a schnauzer's coat to get matted. A summer swim, a roll in autumn leaves, a romp in the snow or a springtime tussle with his canine buddies can turn him into a bramble bush in short order.

After removing a tick, clean your dog's skin with hydro-gen peroxide. If Lyme disease is common where you live, have your veterinarian test the tick. Tick preventive medication will discourage ticks from attaching and kill any that do.

— groomer Andrea Vilardi from West Paterson, N.J.

The Mini's pattern is the same whether stripped or clipped. In the grooming shop, the body is usually clipped with a close-cutting blade unless the coat is very hard or thin, in which case it is left slightly longer. Clipping with the lie (the direction of growth) of the coat, the blade is taken down the sides of the rib cage to a point about even with the elbows. This lie rises diagonally from front to back, where the loin meets the back leg in the tuck-up area.

Clipper work is subtly blended with thinning shears.

The hind legs are cleanly clipped from the thigh to a point above the hock, emphasizing this breed's musculature and angulated legs. Furnishings on all four legs are scissored round to give a "barber pole" effect, with the feet trimmed round and tight to blend perfectly without the toes or nails showing.

The dog's jaunty rear end should be neatly clipped and tidy. Hair growth on the butterfly, the area where the hair swirls on both sides beneath the tail, is clipped against the grain. The private area is clipped clean to keep it sanitary and the belly shaved closely as well.

The neck is clipped to a point just above the breastbone. This breed should never sport a big fluffy bib; his lines are short and sharp. Most groomers clip the head against the grain, from the back of the skull to the brow bone. The cheeks are also clipped forward to the corner of the eye, then to a point midway between the cheek mole and the corner of the mouth. Those fabulous eyebrows are combed forward, then cut at an angle, longest at the innermost point, and carefully blended into the skull with thinning shears. Ears are clipped clean, then carefully trimmed with straight scissors.

The whiskers are shaped at the sides, but the beard should not be trimmed. A knowledgeable groomer will not make it look like a poodle mustache. The head should appear rectangular and the body square. Skilled groomers will adapt the dog's haircut to show off his good points and minimize his flaws but will always stick to this same basic pattern, whether clipping or stripping. To locate a good groomer for your buddy, ask your schnauzer-owning friends, your breeder or look for a certified master groomer on the breed parent club's website.

BETWEEN SALON STOP-INS

Because schnauzer coats are always growing, most owners take them to the groomer every four to six weeks. Between appointments, your job at home is to keep those feathers (the long fingers of hair on your schnauzer's face, ears and body) brushed, so the groomer will not be faced with the prospect of shaving your dog down to the skin. This breed's hair is so fine and silky that it can become too matted to brush out, especially once the coat has been clipped. In such cases, the humane thing to do is to clip the coat down and grow it out. An owner's vanity may suffer, but hours of pulling and tugging a tangled coat on the grooming table is not pleasant for the dog or groomer. Dematting is time-consuming for the groomer and usually costly as well, so it's absolutely necessary to groom your schnauzer daily.

Grooming time provides the perfect opportunity for you to examine your Miniature Schnauzer from head to tail, monitoring his health as well as his appearance. Your dog will soon look forward to this special time with you.

YOUR GROOMING TOOLBOX

To care for your schnauzer's coat, you will need your slicker, a double-sided stainless steel comb with both wide and narrow teeth, a small pair of nail cutters, styptic powder, ear cleaner and ear powder. Dematting tools with replaceable blades are a boon in removing mats and tangles, but they must be used very carefully. Have your groomer demonstrate their proper use. It also helps to keep a spray bottle of waterless shampoo on hand for touch-ups between baths.

To ease into a grooming regimen, begin by stroking your dog's body, speaking softly and reassuringly as you gently massage him all over. Tickle his belly, pat his head and rub his back. These are the areas where puppies love to be touched. Move on to the feet, playing with his paws, touching his toenails and rubbing the pads to desensitize your dog for future nail trimming before he declares his paws off-limits.

Handle your schnauzer's ears, too. Clipping and cleaning them will be a regular part of the grooming routine. Also open his mouth and examine his teeth. This will make your dog less fearful and more co-operative when it is time for vet visits and tooth brushing.

It's much easier to groom your dog on a raised surface. It's also kinder to your back. Relatively inexpensive, lightweight and easy to fold and store, a grooming table is a worthwhile investment. You are more in control with your dog on the table that professionals use (with its attached noose and post) but a countertop or workbench can also fill the bill. There should be room for your

Beard brushing is a part of Mini life!

dog to stand comfortably, but not enough to let him roam around. It helps to have a rubber mat under your schnauzer's feet to provide a nonskid surface.

It is a good idea to leave the leash and collar on for these first sessions, to establish your own control and to help train your puppy. Never leave a dog, especially a puppy, unattended on a table or countertop ; he must be protected from injury and must also absorb the message that you are in charge.

Pick up your puppy with one hand under his chest, the other under his back end, never squeezing his tummy or lifting him by

the scruff of the neck. Place your Mini on the table for a few moments each day, practicing his newly mastered sit and stay cues. If your furry friend is too rambunctious, you may need the help of a partner to help him stand still and prevent him from jumping.

BRUSHING UP

Brushing not only eliminates mats, but also stimulates natural oils that keep the coat lustrous and skin healthy.

Even if it's just for a few minutes a day, brush your schnauzer with a gentle slicker brush, one with flexible straight wire bristles attached to a rubber backing, praising your dog as you make your way through his fluffy puppy coat. Gently but firmly make him stay still, either holding him in your lap or standing him on a table or countertop. Chewing on your fingers or the brush is a no-no; such behavior should be nipped in the bud (pardon the pun!).

Brush over his body a few times a week, beginning at the same point each time. Using such a routine, you are less likely to miss any areas. Begin at the bottom of a rear leg, brushing the hair up and out, one small section at a time. Sometimes called "line brushing," this method involves working your way though the coat inch by inch, up the legs and back down again. Be careful not to dig the metal bristles into your schnauzer's tender skin as you brush. This can create an abrasion called "slicker burn," a painful irritation for your pet. Detangling spray can make your job easier if you mist the coat prior to brushing.

A properly groomed Mini can take your breath away.

Carefully lifting each front leg, brush the armpit area, a favorite hiding spot for mats. Holding your schnauzer's two front paws in one hand, stand him up on his back feet, so you can brush his belly. On the head, carefully brush the eyebrows forward and do the same with the beard. It may help to hold half the beard in one hand while you brush the other half, but be careful not to pull too hard! Next, check your work with your comb, going over every inch of the dog's body to make sure you got rid of all snarls and tangles.

BATH TIME

If you are washing your Mini Schnauzer at home, he must be thoroughly brushed out before and after the bath. Once you add water, mats left in his coat tend to increase and multiply.

You may bathe your dog as often as necessary as long as you use a quality pet shampoo and rinse well. For pups, a tearless product works best. For adults, a protein shampoo gives the coat luster and manageability while a shampoo with bluing makes white furnishings and silver coats sparkle. There are even shampoos for black coats that give your dog the sharpness of a silhouette in motion and remove any rusty areas caused by sunshine or saliva.

Once you've purchased all of your grooming tools, assemble them before bathing your schnauzer. You will need your brush and comb, soft towels, shampoo, a crème rinse (if furnishings mat easily) and a blow dryer. A rubber mat on the bottom of the basin or sink will help your dog keep his footing.

Place your dog in a sink containing a few inches of tepid water, testing the temperature to make sure it's not too hot or cold. Feed additional water into the coat with a gentle spray, beginning at the rear so you won't startle your dog. Put some shampoo in your hand, and massage it into the coat. Pay particular attention to the beard and feet. When washing the facial area, be careful not to get shampoo into your schnauzer's eyes or ears, and do not let him ingest any soap or water.

If administering a flea treatment or medicated bath, leave the lather on the coat for a full 15 minutes, then rinse very thoroughly until your dog's coat feels squeaky clean. If you plan to give a conditioning rinse, make sure your product is well diluted; a little goes

Bath time doesn't have to be a chore; make it fun and pleasant with lots of praise and maybe a treat.

Did You Know? The crunchiness of dry dog food will help keep your Miniature Schnauzer's teeth healthy by reducing the accumulation of plaque and massaging her gums.

a long way. Pour some onto the legs and beard, and then rinse once more.

Some owners like to sponge bathe their Schnauzers between grooming visits, washing only their beards, legs and feet. These little dogs love to hug and kiss, not a pleasant experience if they are packing old foodstuffs in their beards or have bad breath from dental problems.

Wrap your schnauzer in a soft towel and relocate him to your table. Blot the coat; rubbing it every which way will create snarls and tangles in the process. Run the wide end of your comb through the coat before you begin blow-drying from the skin out, brushing as you go to fluff up those furnishings. Be careful not to hold the dryer on one spot too long — that sensitive schnauzer skin can easily burn. Always comb your dog's eyebrows forward as you dry the head area so they won't turn into comical cowlicks. Guard against chills by not letting your schnauzer out in cold weather while he is still damp from the bath.

SPEAKING OF FLEAS ...

Your schnauzer may need weekly flea baths throughout flea season, late summer and early fall. Fortunately, today you can administer a monthly pill to prevent fleas from reproducing or apply one of the topical treatments that work through the coat oils, providing protection for as long as three months. A high-quality flea collar will also prevent them from hopping back on board.

And hop they do: It's estimated that a flea can jump 350 times its body length, comparable to a human jumping the length of a football field!

If you see fleas or their telltale debris, which looks like black pepper, a flea bath is in order. Fleas do more than cause itching and skin damage. They also carry tapeworms, which can debilitate your dog's health by interfering with his ability to gain nourishment from his food.

Many groomers are steering clear from the harsh chemical dips of the past. For the pet's safety and our own, we now use shampoos with more natural flea killers such as pyrethrin, derived from chrysanthemum plants. Other natural flea-killers are neem, melaleuca (Australian tea tree oil), d-limonene a (byproduct of citrus peel) and pennyroyal, another botanical substance (not recommended for nursing female dogs or puppies less than 12 weeks).

Such products get a synergistic boost from permethrin, a synthetic pyrethrin that delivers a longer-lasting, flea-killing effect. To eliminate fleas, your home must also be treated with foggers, carpet powders or the services of a professional exterminator. Fleas reproduce at an alarming rate and can dwell happily in your house all year long.

SMART TIP!

Whichever method of grooming is used, your dog will need regular brushing to prevent mats, especially on the legs and in the beard where food and saliva often turn into solid tangles. Minis love to kiss, not a pleasant experience if they are packing old foodstuffs in their beards or have bad breath from dental problems.

Check your pet for ticks, which are much larger parasites that attach themselves to the skin and carry a host of diseases harmful to both dogs and humans. Before they attach, ticks look like small spiders, but once they start feasting on their host's blood supply, they can bloat up to the size of a grape. Never pull them out with your bare hands. Wear latex gloves and use tweezers to remove their mouthparts from the skin. Drop these little bloodsuckers into a container of alcohol, or dip, to kill them. If they leave a red, swollen spot on your pet, wash the spot with hydrogen peroxide, and apply a dab of antibacterial ointment to heal the bite.

As is the case with medicated shampoos, the lather from flea and tick shampoos should be left on a full 15 minutes. Rinsing thoroughly is absolutely imperative. Shampoo residue left in the coat will only make a skin condition worse.

ODDS AND ENDS

The corners of your schnauzer's eyes should be wiped daily with a tissue or cotton ball dampened with warm water. Matter that accumulates there can irritate the skin and give off a foul odor. Your schnauzer's eyes should be clear and bright, not bloodshot or teary.

At least once a week, you should also clean your dog's ears. Mini Schnauzers sprout hair in their ear canals. For healthy ears, hair should be removed; plucking it with your fingers is the easiest way. Sprinkle a little ear powder inside the ear to make it easier for you to grab the hair and pull it out. This powder also helps keep the ear dry to prevent bacterial infection.

Start with the longer hairs, pulling a few at a time. Don't grab a big clump; this will hurt the dog. Some groomers use hemostats (a type of locking forceps) for this procedure, but if you do, be careful not to pinch your dog's ear cartilage or poke too deeply inside his ears. Follow up by swabbing the powder and ear wax from the ear canal with a cotton ball moistened with an over-the-counter ear cleaner or a homemade solution of half vinegar and half rubbing alcohol. A little bit of ear wax is normal, but if you see a dark, crusty substance, a yellowish discharge, red swollen tissue or if the ear has a foul odor, you will need to make a trip to see the veterinarian. Ear cleaning is preventive only; it will not cure an existing infection.

Most breeders will have their pups' ears cropped at around 8 weeks of age before they go to their new homes. If you have your pup's ears cropped, refrain from grooming them for at least 10 days until the ears are healed, then clean them of debris with your most gentle touch.

Start nail clipping with puppies; it'll make it easier when they are adults.

NAILING THINGS DOWN

The best time to clip your dog's nails is immediately after a bath because the water will have softened the nails, and your schnauzer may be tired out and relaxed by the bath. Nail trimming is recommended every two weeks, using nail clippers or a nail grinding tool.

Trimming nails is crucial to maintaining the Miniature Schnauzer's normal foot shape. Long nails can permanently damage a dog's feet; the tight ligaments of round, arched feet will break down more quickly. If your dog's nails are clicking on the floor, they need trimming.

Your schnauzer should be accustomed to having his nails trimmed at an early age because it will be part of your maintenance routine throughout his life. Not only do neatly trimmed nails look nicer, but long nails can unintentionally scratch someone. Also, long nails have a better chance of ripping and bleeding, or causing your schnauzer's toes to spread.

Before you start clipping, make sure you can identify the quick in each nail (the vein in the center of each nail). It will bleed if it is accidentally cut, which will be painful for your dog since the quick contains a web of nerve endings. Keep some type of clotting agent on hand, such as a styptic pencil or powder (the type used for shaving). This will quickly stop the bleeding when applied to the end of the cut nail. Do not panic if this happens, just stop the bleeding and talk soothingly to your dog. Once he has calmed down, move on to the next nail. It is better to clip a little at a time, particularly with dogs who have dark nails, where the quick isn't easily visible.

Hold your dog steady as you begin trimming his nails; you do not want him to make any sudden movements or run away. Talk to him calmly and stroke him as you clip. Holding his foot in your hand, simply take off the end of each nail in one quick clip. You can purchase nail clippers that are specifically made for dogs at pet-supply stores.

There are two predominant types of clippers. One is the guillotine clipper, which is a hole with a blade in the middle. Using this tool, squeeze the handles so that the blade meets the nail and chops it off. It sounds gruesome, and for some dogs, it is utterly intolerable. The other is the scissor-type clipper, which are gentler on the nail. The important thing to make sure of is that the blades on either of these clippers are sharp. Once the nails are at the desired length, use a nail file to smooth the rough

It's a Fact

Dogs can't rinse and spit after a brushing, so doggie toothpaste must be safe for pets to swallow. Always use a toothpaste specially formulated dogs when brushing your Miniature Schnauzer's teeth.

edges so they don't catch on carpeting or outdoor debris.

A third option is a cordless nail grinder fitted with a fine grade (100 grit) sandpaper cylinder. Stone cylinders are more prone to heat buildup and vibration. When grinding,

Take time to thoroughly dry your Mini after a bath; he could get sick or catch a chill.

use a low-speed (5,000 to 10,000 rpm). Hold your dog's paw firmly in one hand, spreading the toes slightly apart. Touch the spinning grinder wheel to the nail tip for one or two seconds without applying pressure. Repeat if necessary to remove the nail tip protruding beyond the quick. Grinders have the added benefit of leaving nails smooth and free of sharp, jagged edges that traditional nail clippers leave behind.

If the procedure becomes more than you can deal with, just remember: Groomers and veterinarians charge a nominal fee to clip nails. By using their services your dog won't spend the night glowering at you.

When inspecting paws, you must check not only your dog's nails but also the pads of his paws. Check to see that the pads have not become cracked and always inspect between the pads to be sure nothing has become lodged there. Depending upon the season, there may be a danger of grass, seeds, thorns or even tar from the road. Butter, by the way, is useful in removing tar from your Miniature Schnauzer's feet.

IT'S THE TOOTH

Like people, Miniature Schnauzers can suffer from dental disease, so experts recommend regular teeth cleanings. Daily brushing is best, but your dog will benefit from having his teeth brushed a few times a week. The teeth should be white and free of yellowish tartar, and the gums should appear healthy and pink. Gums that bleed easily when you perform dental duties may have gingivitis.

The first thing to know is that your puppy probably isn't going to want your fingers in his mouth. Desensitizing your puppy — getting him to accept that you will be looking at and touching his teeth — is the first step to overcoming his resistance. You can begin this as soon as you get your puppy, with the

help of the thing that motivates dogs the most: food.

For starters, let your puppy lick some chicken, vegetable or beef broth off your finger. Then, dip your finger in broth again, and gently insert your finger in the side of your dog's mouth. Touch his side teeth and gums. Several sessions will get your puppy used to having his mouth touched.

Use a toothbrush specifically made for a dog or a fingertip brush to brush your dog's teeth. Hold his mouth with the fingers of one hand, and brush with the other. Use toothpaste formulated for dogs with delectable flavors like poultry and beef. Brush in a circular motion with the brush held at a 45-degree angle to the gum line. Be sure to get the fronts, tops and sides of each tooth.

Check the teeth for signs of plaque, tartar or gum disease, including redness, swelling, foul breath, discolored enamel near the gum line and receding gums. If you see these, immediately take your Miniature Schnauzer to the veterinarian.

REWARD A JOB WELL DONE

Rewarding your Miniature Schnauzer for behaving well during grooming is the best way to ensure stress-free grooming throughout his lifetime. Playing with your Mini after his brush and bath is the best way to reward your schnauzer for a job well done.

Six Tips for Schnauzer Care

1. Grooming tools can be scary to some dogs, so let yours see and sniff everything at the start. Keep your beauty sessions short, too. Most schnauzers don't enjoy standing still for too long.

2. Look at your dog's eyes for any discharge, and her ears for inflammation, debris or foul odor. If you notice anything that doesn't look right, immediately contact your veterinarian.

3. Choose a time to groom your dog when you don't have to rush, and assemble all of the grooming tools before you begin. This way you can focus on your dog's needs instead of having to stop in the middle of the session to search for an item.

4. Start establishing a grooming routine the day after you bring her home. A regular grooming schedule will make it easier to remember what touch-ups your dog needs.

5. Proper nail care helps with your dog's gait and spinal alignment. Nails that are too long can force a dog to walk improperly. Also, long nails can snag and tear, causing painful injury to your Miniature Schnauzer.

6. Good dental health prevents gum disease and early tooth loss. Brush your schnauzer's teeth daily and take her to the vet yearly.

Six Questions to Ask a Groomer

1. Do you cage dry? Are you willing to hand dry or air dry my pet?

2. What type of shampoo are you using? Is it tearless? If not, do you have a tearless variety available for use?

3. Will you restrain my pet if she acts up during nail clipping? What methods do you use to handle difficult dogs?

4. Are you familiar with the Miniature Schnauzer? Do you have any references from other schnauzer owners?

5. Is the shop air-conditioned during hot weather?

6. Will my dog be getting brushed or just bathed?

TRY THIS

TRAIN

Reward-based training methods — clicking and luring — instruct dogs on what to do and help them do it correctly, setting them up for success and rewards rather than mistakes and punishment. A clicker is a small, plastic device that makes a sharp clicking sound when a button is pressed. You can purchase them at any pet-supply store.

Clicker training is a precise way to mark a desired behavior so an animal knows exactly what behavior earned a reward. Using a clicker, you "charge" the clicker by clicking and giving your Miniature Schnauzer a treat several times, until he understands that the click means a treat is forthcoming. The click then becomes a secondary reinforcer. It's not the reward itself, but it will become so closely linked in your dog's mind with a reward that it has the same effect.

Next, you click the clicker when your Miniature Schnauzer does any desirable behavior. Then, you follow it up with a click and treat. The click exactly marks, more precisely than a word or gesture, the desired behavior, quickly teaching your dog which behaviors will earn rewards.

Did You Know?

The prime period for socialization is short. Most behavior experts agree that positive experiences during the 10-week period between 4 and 14 weeks of age are vital to the development of a puppy who'll grow into an adult dog with a sound temperament.

Most dogs find food rewards meaningful; Miniature Schnauzers are no exception as they tend to be food motivated. This works well because positive training relies on using treats, at least initially, to encourage your dog to demonstrate a certain behavior. The treat is then given as a reward. When you reinforce desired behaviors with rewards that are valuable to your dog, you are met with happy cooperation rather than resistance.

Positive reinforcement does not necessarily equal passivity. While you are rewarding your Miniature Schnauzer's desirable behaviors, you must still manage him to be sure he isn't getting rewarded for his undesirable behaviors. Training tools, such as leashes, tethers, baby gates and crates, help keep your dog out of trouble. The use of force-free negative punishment (the dog's behavior makes a good thing go away) helps him realize there are negative consequences for inappropriate behaviors.

LEARNING SOCIAL GRACES

Now that you have done all of the preparatory work and have helped your Miniature Schnauzer get accustomed to his new home and family, it's time for you to have some fun! Socializing your tiny pup gives you the opportunity to show off your new friend, and your Miniature Schnauzer gets to reap the benefits of being an adorable little creature whom people will want to pet and gush over how precious he is.

Besides getting to know his new family, your puppy should be exposed to other people, animals and situations; but of course, he must not come into close contact with dogs who you don't know well until he has had all his vaccinations. Socialization will help him become well-adjusted as he grows up and less prone to being timid or fearful of the new things he will encounter.

Your Miniature Schnauzer pup's socialization began at the breeder's home, but now it is your responsibility to continue it. The socialization he receives up until he is 12 weeks of age is the most critical, as this is the time when he forms his impressions of the outside world. Be especially careful during the 8- to 10-week period, also known as the fear period. The interaction he receives during this time should be gentle and reassuring. Lack of socialization can manifest itself in fear and aggression as your Miniature Schnauzer matures. Puppies require a lot of human contact, affection, handling and exposure to other animals.

Once your schnauzer has received his necessary vaccinations, feel free to take him out and about (on his leash, of course). Walk him around the neighborhood, take him on your daily errands, let people pet him and let him meet other dogs and pets. Make sure to expose your Miniature Schnauzer to different people — men, women, kids, babies, men with beards, teenagers with cell phones or riding skateboards, joggers, shoppers, someone in a wheelchair, a pregnant woman, etc. Make sure your Miniature Schnauzer explores different surfaces like sidewalks, gravel and even a puddle. Positive experience is the key to building confidence. It's up to you to make sure your Miniature Schnauzer safely discov-

The best way to get your Miniature Schnauzer socialized is to introduce her to different kinds of people and situations. Take her to a restaurant; visit the mall, introduce her to a bearded man and petite lady. Go online to download a socialization checklist at **DogChannel.com/Club-Schnauzer**

ers the world so he will be a calm, confident and well-socialized dog.

It's important that you take the lead in all socialization experiences and never put your pup in a scary or potentially harmful situation. Be mindful of your Miniature Schnauzer's limitations. Fifteen minutes at a public market is fine; two hours at a loud outdoor concert is too much. Meeting vaccinated, tolerant and gentle older dogs is great. Meeting dogs who you don't know or trust isn't a great idea, especially if they appear very energetic, dominant or fearful. Control the situations in which you place your puppy.

The best way to socialize your puppy to a new experience is to make him think it's the best thing ever. You can do this with a lot of happy talk, enthusiasm and yes, food. To convince your puppy that almost any experience is a blast, always carry treats. Consider carrying two types — his puppy chow, which you can give him when introducing him to nonthreatening experiences, and a bag of high-value, mouth-watering treats to give him when introducing him to unfamiliar experiences.

SMART TIP!

If your schnauzer refuses to sit with both haunches squarely beneath her and instead sits on one side or the other, she may have a physical reason for doing so. Discuss the habit with your veterinarian to be certain your dog isn't suffering from some structural problem.

BASIC CUES

All Miniature Schnauzers, regardless of your training and relationship goals, need to know at least five basic good-manner behaviors: sit, down, stay, come and heel. Here are tips for teaching your schnauzer these important cues.

SIT: Every dog should learn to sit.

● Hold a treat at the end of your Miniature Schnauzer's nose.

Socialize your Mini to other dog breeds as a puppy.

Training works best when incorporated into daily life. When your schnauzer asks for something — food, play or whatever else — cue her to do something for you first. Reward her by granting her request. Practice in different settings, so your Mini learns to listen regardless of her surroundings.

- Move the treat over his head.
- When your dog sits, click or say "Yes!"
- Feed your dog the treat.
- If your dog jumps up, hold the treat lower. If he backs up, back him into a corner and wait until he sits. Be patient. Keep your clicker handy, and click (or say "Yes!") and treat anytime he offers a sit.
- When he easily offers sits, say "sit" just before he offers, so he can make the association between the word and the behavior. Add the sit cue when you know you can get the behavior. Your dog doesn't know what the word means until you repeatedly associate it with the appropriate behavior.
- When your schnauzer sits easily on cue, start using intermittent reinforcement by clicking some sits but not others. At first, click most sits and skip an occasional one (this is a high rate of reinforcement). Gradually make your clicks random.

DOWN: If your Miniature Schnauzer can sit, then he can learn to lie down.

- ◆ Have your Miniature Schnauzer sit.
- ◆ Hold the treat in front of his nose. Move it down slowly, straight toward the floor (toward his toes). If he follows all the way down, click and treat.
- ◆ If he gets stuck, move the treat down more slowly. Click and treat for small movements downward — moving his head a bit lower, or inching one paw forward. Keep clicking and treating until your Miniature Schnauzer is all the way down. This training method is called shaping — rewarding small pieces of a behavior until your dog succeeds.
- ◆ If your dog stands as you move the treat toward the floor, have him sit, and move the treat even more slowly downward, shaping with clicks and treats for small, downward movements. If he stands, cheerfully say "Oops!" (which means "Sorry, no treat for that!"), have him sit and try again.
- ◆ If shaping isn't working, sit on the floor with your knee raised. Have your Miniature Schnauzer sit next to you. Put your hand with the treat under your knee and lure him under your leg so he lies down and crawls to follow the treat. Click and treat!
- ◆ When you can lure the down easily, add the verbal cue, wait a few seconds to let your dog think, then lure to show him the association. Repeat until your Miniature Schnauzer goes down on the verbal cue; then begin using intermittent reinforcement.

STAY: What good are sit and down cues if your dog doesn't stay?

- ▲ Start with your Miniature Schnauzer in a sit or down position.
- ▲ Put the treat in front of your dog's nose and keep it there.
- ▲ Click and reward several times while he is in position, then release him with a cue you will always use to tell him the stay is over. Common release cues are: "all done," "break," "free," "free dog," "at ease" and "OK."
- ▲ When your Miniature Schnauzer will stay in a sit or down position while you click and treat, add your verbal stay cue. Say

With the proper training, your schnauzer will be as well behaved as she is adorable. One certification that all dogs should receive is the American Kennel Club Canine Good Citizen, which rewards dogs with good manners. Go to **DogChannel.com/Club-Schnauzer** and click on "Downloads" to get the 10 steps required for your dog to be a CGC.

▲ When he will stay for 15 to 20 seconds, add small distractions: shuffling your feet, moving your arms and small hops. Gradually increase distractions. If your Miniature Schnauzer makes mistakes, it means you're adding too much, too fast.

▲ When he'll stay for 15 to 20 seconds with distractions, gradually add distance. Have your Miniature Schnauzer stay, take a half-step back, click, return and treat. When he'll stay with a half-step, tell him to stay, take a full step back, click and return. Always return to your dog to treat after you click, but before you release. If you always return, his stay becomes strong. If you call him to you, his stay gets weaker due to his eagerness to come to you.

COME: A reliable recall — coming when called — can be a challenging behavior to teach. It is possible, however. To succeed, you need to install an automatic response to your "come" cue — one so automatic that your Miniature Schnauzer doesn't even stop to think when he hears it, but will spin on his heels and charge to you at full speed.

■ Start by charging a come cue the same way you charged your clicker. If your Miniature Schnauzer already ignores the word "come," pick a different cue, like "front" or "hugs." Say your cue and feed him a bit of scrumptious treat. Repeat this until his eyes light up when he hears the cue. Now you're ready to start training.

■ With your Miniature Schnauzer on a leash, run away and cheerfully call out your charged cue. When he follows, click; feed him a treat when he reaches you. For a more enthusiastic come, run away at full speed as you call him. When he follows, stop running, click and give him a treat. The better your

"stay," pause for a second or two, click and say "stay" again. Release.

▲ When your Miniature Schnauzer is getting the idea, say "stay," whisk the treat out of sight behind your back, click the clicker and whisk the treat back. Be sure to get the treat all the way to his nose, so he does not jump up. Gradually increase the duration of the stay.

it's a Fact

Behaviors are best trained by breaking them down into their simplest components, teaching those and then linking them together to end up with the complete behavior. Keep treats small so you can reward many times without stuffing your schnauzer. Remember, don't bore your schnauzer; avoid excessive repetition.

Miniature Schnauzer gets at coming, the farther away he can be when you call him.

SMART TIP!

If you begin teaching the heel cue by taking long walks and letting your dog pull you along, she may misinterpret this action as acceptable. When you pull back on the leash to counteract her pulling, she will read that tug as a signal to pull even harder!

■ Once your Miniature Schnauzer understands the come cue, play with more people, each holding a clicker and treats. Stand a short distance apart and take turns calling and running away. Click and treat in turn as he comes to each of you. Gradually increase the distance until he comes flying to each person from a distance.

■ When you and your Mini Schnauzer are ready to practice in wide-open spaces, attach a long — a 20- to 50-foot — leash to your dog, so that you can get a hold of him if that taunting squirrel nearby is too much of a temptation. If he does get distracted, head to a practice area where there are less tempting distractions.

HEEL: Heeling means that your dog can calmly walk beside you without pulling. It takes time and patience on your part to succeed at teaching your dog that you will not proceed unless he is walking beside you with ease. Pulling out ahead on the leash is definitely unacceptable.

● Begin by holding the leash in your left hand as your Miniature Schnauzer sits beside your left leg. Move the loop end of the leash to your right hand but keep your left hand short on the leash so it keeps your dog close to you.

● Say "heel" and step forward on your left foot. Keep your Miniature Schnauzer close to you and take three steps. Stop and have your dog sit next to you in what we now call the heel position. Praise verbally, but do not touch your dog. Hesitate a moment and begin again with "heel," taking three steps and stopping, at which point your dog is told to sit again.

Your goal here is to have your dog walk those three steps without pulling on the leash. Once he will walk calmly beside you for three steps without pulling, increase the number of steps you take to five. When he will walk politely beside you while you take five steps, you can increase the length of your walk to 10 steps. Keep increasing the length of your stroll until your dog will walk beside you without pulling for as long as you want him to heel. When you stop heeling, indicate to the dog that the exercise is over by petting him and saying "OK, good dog." The "OK" is used as a release word, meaning that the exercise is finished, and he is free to relax.

● If you are dealing with a Miniature Schnauzer who insists on pulling you around, simply put on your brakes and stand your ground until your Miniature Schnauzer realizes that the two of you are not going anywhere until he is beside you and moving at your pace, not his. It may take some time just standing there to convince your dog that you are the leader, and you will be the one to decide on the direction and speed of your travel.

● Each time your schnauzer looks up at you or slows down to give a slack leash between the two of you, quietly praise him and say, "Good heel. Good dog." Eventually, your Miniature Schnauzer will begin to respond, and within a few days he will be walking politely beside you without pulling on the leash. At first, the training sessions should be kept short and very positive; soon your schnauzer will be able to walk nicely with you for increasingly longer distances. A smart owner will remember to give their dog free time and the opportunity to run and play when you have finished heel practice.

LEAVE IT ALONE

Miniature Schnauzers enjoy eating, which makes it easy to train them using treats. But there's a downside to their gastronomic gusto — some Miniature Schnauzers will gobble down anything even remotely edible. This could include fresh food, rotten food, things that once were food and any item that's ever been in contact with food. So, if you don't want your Miniature Schnauzer gulping trash, teach him to leave things alone when told.

Place a tempting tidbit on the floor and cover it with your hand (gloved against teeth, if necessary). Say your cue word ("leave it" or "nah"). Your dog might lick, nibble and paw your hand; don't give in or you'll be rewarding bad manners.

Did You Know?

Once your schnauzer understands what behavior goes with a specific cue, it is time to start weaning her off the food treats. At first, give a treat after each exercise. Then, start to give a treat only after every other exercise. Mix up times when you offer a food reward and when you only offer praise. This way your dog will never know when she is going to receive food and praise, or only praise.

Wait until he moves away, then click or praise, and give a treat. Do not let your dog eat the food that's on the floor, only the treats you give him. Repeat until your Miniature Schnauzer stops moving toward the tempting food.

Lift your hand momentarily, letting your dog see the temptation. Say the cue word. Be ready to protect the treat but instantly reward him if he resists temptation. Repeat, moving your hand farther away and waiting longer before clicking and rewarding.

Increase the difficulty gradually; practice in different locations, add new temptations, drop treats from standing height, drop several at a time and step away.

Remember to use your cue word, so your dog will know what he's expected to do. Always reward good behavior! Rehearse this skill daily for a week. After that, you'll have enough real-life opportunities to practice.

TRAINING TIPS

If not properly socialized and trained, even a well-bred Miniature Schnauzer will exhibit bad behaviors such as jumping up, barking, chasing, chewing and other destructive behaviors. You can prevent these habits and help your Miniature Schnauzer become the perfect dog you've wished for by following some basic training and behavior guidelines.

Be consistent. Consistency is important, not just in terms of what you allow your Miniature Schnauzer to do (get on the sofa, perhaps) and not do (jump up on people), but also in the verbal and body language cues you use with your dog and in his daily routine.

Be gentle but firm. Positive training methods are very popular. Properly applied, dog-friendly methods are wonderfully effec-

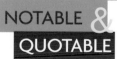

NOTABLE & QUOTABLE

If you want to make your dog happy, create a digging spot where she's allowed to disrupt the earth. Encourage her to dig there by burying bones and toys, and helping her dig them up. — Pat Miller, a certified dog trainer and owner of Peaceable Paws dog-training facility in Hagerstown, Md.

TIME TO TRAIN | 135

tive, creating canine-human relationships based on respect and cooperation.

Manage behavior. All living things, including dogs, repeat behaviors that are rewarded. Behaviors that aren't reinforced will go away.

Provide adequate exercise. A tired Mini is a well-behaved schnauzer. Many behavior problems can be avoided, others resolved, by providing your Miniature Schnauzer with enough exercise.

THE THREE-STEP PROGRAM

Perhaps it's too late to give your dog consistency, training and management from the start. Maybe he came from a Miniature Schnauzer rescue shelter or you didn't realize the importance of these basic guidelines when he was a puppy. He already may have learned some bad behaviors. Perhaps they're even part of his genetic package. Many problems can be modified with ease using the following three-step process for changing an unwanted behavior.

Step No. 1: Visualize the behavior you want your dog to exhibit. If you simply try to stop your Miniature Schnauzer from doing something, you leave a behavior vacuum. You need to fill that vacuum with something, so your dog doesn't return to the same behavior or fill it with one that's even worse! If you're tired of your dog jumping up, decide what you'd prefer instead. A dog who greets people by sitting politely in front of them is a joy to own.

Step No. 2: Prevent your schnauzer from being rewarded for the behavior you don't want him to exhibit. Management to the rescue! When your Miniature Schnauzer jumps up to greet you or get your attention, turn your back and step away to show him that jumping up no longer works in gaining your attention.

Step No. 3: Generously reinforce the desired behavior. Keep in mind that dogs will repeat behaviors that generate rewards. If your Miniature Schnauzer no longer gets attention for jumping up and is heavily reinforced with attention and treats for sitting, he will offer sits instead of jumping, because he's learned that sitting will get him what he wants.

COUNTER CONDITIONING

The three-step program helps to correct those behaviors that temporarily gives your Mini satisfaction. For example, he jumps up to get attention; he countersurfs because he finds good food on counters; he nips to get you to play with him.

The steps don't work well when you're dealing with behaviors that are based in strong emotion, such as aggression and fear, or with hardwired behaviors such as chasing prey. With these, you can change the emotional or hardwired response through counter conditioning — programming a new emotional or automatic response to the stimulus by giving it a new association. Here's how you would counter condition a Miniature Schnauzer who chases after skateboarders while you're walking him on a leash.

NOTABLE & QUOTABLE *Be careful in the timing of your treats. A common mistake is to reward at the wrong time. If you reach in your pocket for a food treat and your dog gets up, do not give a treat. Otherwise, he will interpret you reaching in your pocket for complying with the stay cue.* — Judy Super, a professional dog trainer in Minneapolis, Minn.

1. Have a large supply of high-value treats, such as canned chicken.

2. Station yourself with your Miniature Schnauzer on a leash at a location where skateboarders will pass by at a subthreshold distance X — that is, where your Miniature Schnauzer is alerted to the approaching person but doesn't bark.

3. Wait for a skateboarder. The instant your Mini notices the skateboarder, feed him bits of chicken, nonstop, until the skateboarder is gone. Stop feeding him.

4. Repeat many times until, when the skateboarder appears, your Mini looks at you with a big grin as if to say, "Yay! Where's my chicken?" This is a conditioned emotional response, or CER.

5. When you have a consistent CER at distance X, decrease the distance slightly, perhaps minus 1 foot, and repeat until you consistently get the CER at this distance.

6. Continue decreasing the distance and obtaining a CER at each level, until a skateboarder zooming right past your Miniature Schnauzer elicits the "Where's my chicken?" response. Now go back to distance X and add a second skateboarder. Continue this process of desensitization until your Mini doesn't turn a hair at a bevy of skateboarders.

Even the best dogs have some bad habits. If you are frustrated with a particular behavior that your schnauzer exhibits, don't despair! Join Club Schnauzer, where you can ask other Mini owners for advice. Log on to **DogChannel.com/Club-Schnauzer** and click on "Community."

BAD BEHAVIOR

Discipline — training one to act in accordance with rules — brings order to life. It's as simple as that. Without discipline, particularly in a group society, chaos reigns supreme and the group will eventually perish. Humans and canines are social animals and need some form of discipline in order to function effectively. Dogs need discipline in their lives in order to understand how their pack (you and other family members) functions and how they must act in order to survive.

Living with an untrained schnauzer is a lot like owning a piano that you do not know how to play; it is a nice object to look at but it does not do much more than that to bring you pleasure. Now, try taking piano lessons and suddenly the piano comes alive and brings forth magical sounds and rhythms that set your heart singing and your body swaying.

The same is true of your Miniature Schnauzer. Every dog is a big responsibility, and if not sensibly trained may develop

> **Did You Know?**
>
> **Anxiety can make a pup miserable.** Living in a world with scary, monsters and suspected schnauzer-eaters roaming the streets has to be pretty nerve-wracking. The good news is that timid dogs are not doomed to be forever ruled by fear. Owners who understand a timid Miniature Schnauzer's needs can help her build self-confidence and a more optimistic view of life.

unacceptable behaviors that annoy you or cause family friction.

To train your Miniature Schnauzer, you can enroll in an obedience class to teach him good manners as you learn how and why he behaves the way he does. You will also find out how to communicate with your Miniature Schnauzer and how to recognize and understand his communications with you. Suddenly your dog takes on a new role in your life; he is interesting, smart, well-behaved and fun to be with. He demonstrates his bond of devotion to you daily. In other words, your Miniature Schnauzer does wonders for your ego because he constantly reminds you that you are not only his leader, you are his hero!

Those involved with teaching dog obedience and counseling owners about their dogs' behavior have discovered interesting facts about dog ownership. For example, training dogs when they are puppies results in the highest success rate in developing well-mannered and well-adjusted adult. Training an older Miniature Schnauzer, from 6 months to 6 years, can produce almost equal results, providing that the owner accepts the dog's slower learning rate and is willing to patiently work to help him succeed. Unfortunately, many owners of untrained adult dogs lack the patience necessary, so they do not persist until their dogs are successful at learning particular behaviors.

Training a 10- to 16-week-old Miniature

Schnauzer pup (20 weeks maximum) is like working with a dry sponge in a pool of water. The pup soaks up whatever you teach him and constantly looks for more to do and learn. At this early age, his body is not yet producing hormones, and therein lies the reason for such a high success rate. Without hormones, he is focused on you and is not particularly interested in investigating other places, dogs, people, etc.

You are his leader; his provider of food, water, shelter and security. Your Miniature Schnauzer latches onto you and wants to stay close. He usually will follow you from room to room, won't let you out of his sight when you are outdoors with him and will respond in like manner to the people and animals you encounter. If you greet a friend warmly, he will happily greet the person as well. If, however, you are hesitant, even anxious, about the approaching stranger, he will also respond accordingly.

Once your puppy begins to produce hormones, his natural curiosity emerges and he begins to investigate the world around him. It is at this time when you may notice your untrained dog begins to wander away and ignore your cues to stay close.

There are usually training classes within a reasonable distance of your home, but you also can do a lot to train your dog yourself. Sometimes classes are available but the tuition is too costly, whatever the circumstances, information about training your Miniature without formal obedience classes lies within the pages of this book.

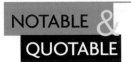

NOTABLE & QUOTABLE

The best way to get through to dogs is through their stomach and mind — not the use of force. You have to play a mind game with them.

— *Sara Gregware, a professional dog handler and trainer in Goshen, Conn.*

If the recommended procedures are followed faithfully, you can expect positive results that will prove rewarding for both you and your dog.

Whether your new schnauzer is a pup or a mature adult, the teaching methods and training techniques used in basic behaviors are the same. No dog, whether puppy or adult, likes harsh or inhumane training methods. All creatures, however, respond favorably to gentle motivational methods and sincere praise and encouragement.

The following behavioral issues are those most commonly encountered. Remember, every dog and situation is unique. Because behavioral abnormalities are the leading

SMART TIP!

The golden rule of dog training is simple. For each question (cue), there is only one correct answer (reaction). One cue equals one reaction. Keep practicing the cue until your dog reacts correctly without hesitation. Be repetitive but not monotonous. Dogs get bored just as people do; a bored dog's attention will not be focused on the lesson.

reason for owners' abandoning their pets, we hope that you will make a valiant effort to solve your Miniature Schnauzer's behavioral issues.

Stay consistent with your Mini's training to yield the best results. A well-trained dog has a happy owner.

NIP NIPPING

As puppies start to teethe, they feel the need to sink their teeth into anything — unfortunately that includes your fingers, arms, hair, toes, whatever happens to be available. You may find this behavior cute for about the first five seconds — until you feel just how sharp those puppy teeth are.

Nipping is something you want to discourage immediately and consistently with a firm "No!" (or whatever number of firm "nos" it takes for your dog to understand that you mean business) and replace your finger with an appropriate chew toy.

STOP THAT WHINING

A puppy will often cry, whine, whimper, howl or make some type of commotion when he is left alone. This is basically his way of calling out for attention, of calling out to make sure that you know he is there and that you have not forgotten about him. He feels insecure when he is left alone; for example, when you are out of the house and he is in his crate, or when you are in another part of the house and he cannot see you.

The noise he is making is an expression of the anxiety he feels at being alone, so he needs to be taught that being alone is OK. You are not actually training your Miniature Schnauzer to stop making noise, you are training him to feel comfortable when he is alone and thus removing the need to make the noise.

This is where his crate with a cozy blanket and a toy comes in handy. You want to know that your pup is safe when you are not there to supervise the best place for him to be is in his crate, rather than roaming about the house. In order for your pup to stay in his crate without making a fuss, he needs to be comfortable there. On that note, it is extremely important that the crate is never used as a form of punishment, or your Miniature Schnauzer puppy will have a negative association with his crate.

Acclimate your puppy to his crate in short, gradually increasing time intervals. During these periods, put him in the crate, maybe with a treat, and stay in the room with him. If he cries or makes a fuss, do not go to him, but stay in his sight. Gradually, he will realize staying in his crate is all right without your help and it will not be so traumatic for him when you are not around. You may want to leave the radio on softly when you leave the house; the sound of human voices can comfort him.

CHEW ON THIS

The national canine pastime is chewing! Every dog loves to sink his "canines" into a tasty bone, but anything will do! Dogs chew to massage their gums, make their new teeth feel better and exercise their jaws. This is a natural behavior deeply imbedded in all things canine. Owners should not stop their dog's chewing, but redirect it to chew-worthy objects. A smart owner will purchase proper chew toys for their Miniature Schnauzer, like strong nylon bones. Be sure that these devices are safe and durable because your dog's safety is at risk.

Did You Know?

Dogs do not understand our language. They can be trained, however, to react to a certain sound, at a certain volume. Never use your Miniature Schnauzer's name during a reprimand, as she might come to associate it with a bad thing!

Your Miniature Schnauzer may howl, whine or otherwise vocalize her displeasure at your leaving the house and her being left alone. This is a normal case of separation anxiety, but there are things that can be done to eliminate this problem. Your dog needs to learn that she will be fine on her own for a while and that she will not wither away if she isn't attended to every minute of the day.

In fact, constant attention can lead to separation anxiety in the first place. If you are endlessly coddling and cuddling your Miniature Schnauzer, she will come to expect this from you all of the time, and it will be more traumatic for her when you are not there.

To help minimize separation anxiety, make your entrances and exits as low-key as possible. Do not give your schnauzer a long, drawn-out goodbye, and do not lavish her with hugs and kisses when you return. This will only make her miss you more when you are away. Another thing you can try is to give your dog a treat when you leave; this will keep her occupied, her mind off the fact that you just left and help her associate your leaving as a pleasant experience.

You may have to acclimate your schnauzer to being left alone in intervals, much like when you introduced her to her crate. Of course, when your dog starts whimpering as you approach the door, your first instinct will be to run to her and comfort her, but don't do it! Eventually, she will adjust and be just fine — if you take it in small steps. Her anxiety stems from being placed in an unfamiliar situation; by familiarizing her with being alone, she will learn that she will be just fine.

When your Miniature Schnauzer is alone in the house, confine her in her crate or a designated dog-proof area. This should be the area in which she sleeps, so she will already feel comfortable there and this should make her feel more at ease when she is alone. This is just one of the many examples in which a crate is an invaluable tool for you and your Miniature Schnauzer, and another reinforcement of why your dog should view her crate as a happy place of her own.

The best solution is prevention: That is, put your shoes, handbags and other alluring objects in their proper places (out of the reach of the growing canine mouth). Direct puppies to their toys whenever you see them tasting the furniture legs or the leg of your pants. Make a loud noise to attract your Miniature Schnauzer pup's attention and immediately escort him to his chew toy and engage him with the toy for at least four minutes, praising and encouraging him all the while.

NO MORE JUMPING

Jumping is a dog's friendly way of saying hello! Some owners don't mind when their dog jumps, which is fine for them. The problem arises when guests arrive and the dog greets them in the same manner — whether they like it or not! However friendly the greeting may be, chances are your visitors will not appreciate your dog's enthusiasm. Your dog will not be able to distinguish upon whom he can jump and whom he cannot. Therefore, it is probably best to discourage this behavior entirely.

Pick a cue such as "off" (avoid using "down" because you will use that for your dog to lie down) and tell him "off" when he jumps. Place him on the ground on all fours and have him sit, praising him the whole time. Always lavish him with praise and pet-ting when he is in the sit position, that way you are still giving him a warm, affectionate greeting, because you are as pleased to see him as he is to see you!

UNWANTED BARKING MUST GO

Barking is how dogs talk. It can be somewhat frustrating because it is not easy to tell what your dog means by his bark: is he excited, happy, frightened, angry? Whatever it is your dog is trying to say, he should not be punished for barking. It is only when barking becomes excessive, and when excessive barking becomes a bad habit, that the behavior needs to be modified.

If an intruder came into your home in the middle of the night and your dog barked a warning, wouldn't you be pleased? You would probably deem your dog a hero, a wonderful guardian and protector of the home. On the other hand, if a friend unexpectedly drops by, rings the doorbell and is greeted with a sudden sharp bark, you would probably be annoyed at your dog. But isn't it the same behavior? Your dog doesn't know any better … unless he sees who is at the door and it is someone he is familiar with, he will bark as a means of vocalizing that his (and your) territory is being threatened. While your friend is not posing a threat, it is all the same to your dog. Barking is his means of letting you know there is an intruder, whether friend or foe, on your property. This type of barking is instinctive and should not be discouraged.

Excessive, habitual barking, however, is a problem that should be corrected early on. As your Miniature Schnauzer grows up, you will be able to tell when his barking is purposeful and when it is for no reason, you will able to distinguish your dog's different barks and with what they are associated. For example, the bark when someone comes to the door

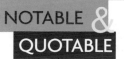

Stage false departures. Pick up your car keys and put on your coat, then put them away and go about your routine. Do this several times a day, ignoring your dog while you do it. Soon, her reaction to these triggers will decrease.

— *September Morn, a dog trainer and behavior specialist in Bellingham, Wash.*

will be different from the bark when he is excited to see you. It is similar to a person's tone of voice, except that your Miniature Schnauzer has to completely rely on tone because he does not have the benefit of using words. An incessant barker will be evident at an early age.

There are some things that encourage barking. For example, if your dog barks non-stop for a few minutes and you give him a treat to quiet him, he believes you are rewarding him for barking. He will now associate barking with getting a treat, and will keep barking until he receives his reward.

FOOD STEALING AND BEGGING

Is your Miniature Schnauzer devising ways of stealing food from your cupboards? If so, you must answer the following questions: Is your dog really hungry? Why is there food on the coffee table? Face it, some dogs are more food-motivated than others; some are totally obsessed by a slab of brisket and can only think of their next meal. Food stealing is terrific fun and always yields a great reward — food, glorious food!

Therefore, the owner's goal is to make the reward less rewarding, even startling! Plant a shaker can (an empty can with a lid and filled with coins) on the table so that it catches your pooch off-guard. There are other devices available that will surprise your dog when he is looking for a mid-afternoon snack. Such remote-control devices, though not the first choice of some trainers, allow the correction to come from the object instead of you. These devices are also useful to keep your snacking Miniature Schnauzer from napping on forbidden furniture.

Just like food stealing, begging is a favorite pastime of hungry pups with the same reward — food! Dogs learn quickly that

No matter how cute, never give in to a beggar!

humans love that feed-me pose and that their owners keep the good food for themselves. Why would humans dine on kibble when they can cook up sausages and kielbasa? Begging is a conditioned response related to a specific stimulus, time and place; the sounds of the kitchen, cans and bottles opening, crinkling bags and the smell of food preparation will excite your chowhound and soon his paws are in the air!

Here is how to stop this behavior: Never give in to a beggar, no matter how appealing or desperate! By giving in, you are rewarding your dog for jumping up, whining and rubbing his nose into you. By ignoring your dog, you eventually will force the behavior into extinction. Note that his behavior will likely get worse before it disappears, so be sure there are not any softies in the family who will give in to your schnauzer every time he whimpers "Please."

DIG THIS

Digging, seen as a destructive behavior by humans, is actually quite a natural behavior in dogs. Their desire to dig can be irrepressible and most frustrating. When digging happens, it is an innate behavior redirected into something the dog can do in his everyday life. In the wild, a dog would be actively seeking food, making his own shelter, etc. He would be using his paws in a purposeful manner for his survival. Because you provide him with food and shelter, he has no need to use his paws for these purposes and so the energy he would be using may manifest itself in the form of holes all over your yard and flower beds.

Perhaps your dog is digging as a reaction to boredom — it is somewhat similar to someone eating a whole bag of chips in front of the TV — because they are there and there is nothing better to do! Basically, the answer

Did You Know? **Some natural remedies for separation anxiety are reputed to have calming effects,** but check with your vet before use. Flower essence remedies are water-based extracts of different plants, which are stabilized and preserved with alcohol. A human dose is only a few drops, so seek advice from a natural healing practitioner on proper dosage for your schnauzer.

is to provide your dog with adequate play and exercise so his mind and paws are occupied, and so he feels as if he is doing something useful.

Of course, digging is easiest to control if it is stopped as soon as possible, but it is often hard to catch your dog in the act. If your Miniature Schnauzer is a compulsive digger and is not easily distracted by other activities, you can designate an area on your property where it is OK for him to dig. If you catch him digging in an off-limits area of the yard, immediately bring him to the approved area and praise him for digging there. Keep a close eye on him so you can catch him in the act; that is the only way to make him understand where digging is permitted and where it is not. If you take him to a hole he dug an hour ago and tell him "no," he will understand that you are not fond of holes, dirt or flowers. If you catch him while he is stifle-deep in your tulips, that is when he will get your message.

POOP ALERT!

Humans find feces eating, aka *coprophagia*, one of the most disgusting behaviors that their dog could engage in; yet to your dog it is perfectly normal. Vets have found that diets with low digestibility, containing relatively low levels of fiber and high levels of starch, increase *coprophagia*. Therefore, high-fiber diets may decrease the likelihood of your dog eating feces. To discourage this behavior, feed nutritionally complete food in the proper amount. If changes in his diet do not seem to work, and no medical cause can be found, you will have to modify his behavior through environmental control before it becomes a habit.

There are some tricks you can try, such as adding an unpleasant-tasting substance to the feces to make them unpalatable or adding something to your dog's food which will make it unpleasant tasting after it passes through your dog. The best way to prevent your dog from eating his stool is to make it unavailable — clean up after he eliminates and remove any stool from the yard. If it is not there, he cannot eat it.

Never reprimand your dog for stool eating, as this rarely impresses your dog. Vets recommend distracting your Miniature Schnauzer while he is in the act. Another option is to muzzle your dog when he goes in the yard to relieve himself; this usually is effective within 30 to 60 days. *Coprophagia* is mostly seen in pups 6 to 12 months, and usually disappears around the dog's first birthday.

AGGRESSION

Aggression, when not controlled, always becomes dangerous. An aggressive schnauzer, no matter the size, may lunge at, bite or even attack a person or another dog. Aggressive behavior is not to be tolerated. It is more than just inappropriate behavior; it is not safe. It is painful for a family to watch their dog become unpredictable in his behavior to the point where they are afraid of him. While not all aggressive behavior is dangerous, growling and baring teeth can be frightening. It is important to ascertain why your dog is acting in this manner. Aggression is a display of dominance, and your dog should not have the dominant role in his pack, which is in this case your family.

It is important not to challenge an aggressive dog, as this could provoke an attack. Observe your Miniature Schnauzer's body language. Does he make direct eye contact and stare? Does he try to make himself as large as possible: ears pricked, chest out, neck arched? Height and size signify authority in a dog pack — being taller or "above" another dog literally means that he is "above" in the social status. These body signals tell you that your Miniature Schnauzer thinks he is in charge, a problem that needs to be addressed. An aggressive dog is unpredictable: You never know when he is going to strike and what he is going to do. You cannot understand why a dog that is playful and loving one minute is growling and snapping the next.

The best solution is to consult a behavioral specialist, one who has experience with Miniature Schnauzers, if possible. Together, perhaps you can pinpoint the cause of your dog's aggression and do something about it. An aggressive dog cannot be trusted and a dog who cannot be trusted is not safe to have as a family pet. If, very unusually, you find

All dogs will bark from time to time, but unwanted, excessive barking can be controlled with training.

that your dog has become untrustworthy and you feel it necessary to seek a new home with a more suitable family and environment, explain fully to the new owners all your reasons for rehoming the dog to be fair to all concerned. In the very worst case, you will have to consider euthanasia.

AGGRESSION TOWARD DOGS

A dog's aggressive behavior toward another dog sometimes stems from insufficient exposure to other dogs at an early age. It is the breeder and owner's responsibility to curb and redirect any signs of aggression so that your Miniature Schnauzer can become an upright member of canine society. If other dogs make your schnauzer nervous and agitated, he might use aggression as a defensive mechanism. A dog who has not received sufficient socialization to other canines tends to believe he is the only dog on the planet. He becomes so dominant that he does not even show signs that he is fearful or threatened. Without growling or any other physical signal as a warning, he will lunge at and bite another dog. A way to correct this is to let your Miniature Schnauzer approach another dog only when walking on a leash. Watch very closely and at the very first sign of aggression, correct your dog and pull him away. Scold him for any sign of discomfort, and praise him when he ignores

NOTABLE & QUOTABLE

The purpose of puppy classes is for puppies to learn how to learn. The pups get the training along the way, but the training is almost secondary.
— professional trainer Peggy Shunick Duezabou of Helena, Mont.

or tolerates the other dog. Keep this up until he stops the aggressive behavior, learns to ignore other dogs or accepts other dogs. Praise him lavishly for his correct behavior.

DOMINANT AGGRESSION

A social hierarchy is firmly established in a wild dog pack; dogs want to dominate those under him and please those above him. They know there must be a leader. If you are not the obvious choice for emperor, your dog will assume the throne! These conflicting, innate desires are what you are up against when training your dog. In training a dog to obey cues, you are reinforcing the fact that you are the top dog in the "pack" and that your dog should, and should want to, serve his superior. Thus, you are suppressing your dog's urge to dominate by modifying his behavior and making him obedient.

An important part of training is taking every opportunity to reinforce that you are the leader. The simple action of making your Miniature Schnauzer sit to wait for his food says you control when he eats and that he is dependent on you for food. Although it may be difficult, do not give in to your dog's wishes every time he whines at you or looks at you with his pleading eyes. It is a constant effort to show your dog that his place in the pack is at the bottom. This is not meant to sound cruel or inhumane. You love your Miniature Schnauzer and you should treat him with care and affection. You certainly did not get a dog just so you could boss around another creature. Dog training is not about being cruel or feeling important, it is about molding your dog's behavior into what is acceptable and teaching him to live by your rules. In theory, it is quite simple: catch him in appropriate behavior and reward him for it. Add a dog into the equation and it becomes a bit more trying, but as a rule of thumb, positive reinforcement works best.

With a dominant dog, punishment and negative reinforcement can have the opposite effect of what you are trying to achieve. It can make your dog fearful and/or act out aggressively if he feels he is being challenged. Remember, a dominant dog perceives himself at the top of the

social heap and will fight to defend his perceived status. The best way to prevent that is to never give him reason to think he is in control in the first place. If you are having trouble training your Miniature Schnauzer and it seems as if he is constantly challenging your authority, seek the help of an obedience trainer or behavioral specialist. A professional will work with both you and your dog to teach you effective techniques to use at home. Beware of trainers who rely on excessively harsh methods; scolding is necessary now and then, but the focus in your training should always be positive reinforcement.

If you can isolate what brings out your Miniature Schnauzer's fear reaction, you can help him get over it. Supervise your schnauzer's interactions with people and other dogs, and praise him when it goes well. If he starts to act aggressively in a situation, correct him and remove him from the situation. Do not let people approach your dog and start petting him without your expressed permission. That way, you can have your dog sit to accept petting and praise him when he behaves appropriately; you are focusing on praise and modifying his behavior by rewarding him. By being gentle and by supervising his interactions, you are showing him that there is no need to be afraid or defensive.

SEXUAL BEHAVIOR

Dogs exhibit certain sexual behaviors that may have influenced your choice of male or female when you first purchased your Miniature Schnauzer. To a certain extent, spaying/neutering will eliminate these behaviors.

Smart Miniature Schnauzer owners must also recognize that mounting is not merely a sexual expression. It is also one of dominance. Be consistent and persistent in your training, and you will find that you can move mounters.

One of the best ways to nurture a cooperative and solid relationship with your Miniature Schnauzer is to become involved in an activity both of you can enjoy. A bored schnauzer can easily become a troublesome dog.

Deciding what recreation activity you and your Miniature Schnauzer would enjoy the most takes some consideration. Do you want a sport, such as agility, where you and your dog are both active participants? Would you prefer an activity, such as flyball, where your dog does most of the running? Does something less physical, such as visiting senior citizens, sound more like your cup of tea? Perhaps a brief synopsis of some of the more popular dog-friendly recreations will help you narrow down the choices.

EXERCISE OPTIONS

All Miniature Schnauzers need exercise to keep them physically and mentally healthy. An inactive dog is an overweight dog, who will likely suffer joint strain or torn ligaments. Inactive dogs also are prone to mischief and may do anything to relieve their boredom. This often leads to behavioral problems, such as chewing or barking. Regular daily exercise, such as walks and play sessions, will keep your Miniature Schnauzer slim, trim and happy.

Did You Know? The Fédération Internationale Cynologique is the world kennel club that governs dog shows in Europe and elsewhere around the world.

Before You Begin
Because of the physical demands of sporting activities, a Miniature Schnauzer puppy shouldn't begin official training until she is done growing. That doesn't mean, though, that you can't begin socializing her to sports. Talk to your veterinarian about what age is appropriate to begin.

Provide your Miniature Schnauzer with interactive play that stimulates his mind as well as his body. It's a good idea to have a daily period of one-on-one play, especially with a puppy or young dog. Continue this type of interaction throughout your dog's life, and you will build a lasting bond. Even senior Miniature Schnauzers need the stimulation that activity provides.

If your Miniature Schnauzer is older or overweight, consult your veterinarian about how much and what type of exercise he needs. Usually, a 10- to 15-minute walk once a day is a good start. As the pounds start to drop off, your dog's energy level will rise, and you can increase the amount of daily exercise.

Whether a dog is trained in the structured environment of a class or alone with his owner at home, there also are many sporting activities that can bring fun and rewards to owner and dog once they have mastered basic training techniques.

AGILITY TRIALS
Agility is a fast-growing sport, attracting dogs of all kinds and their equally diverse owners. In agility, the dog, off leash but guided by the handler, runs a course of obstacles including jumps, tunnels, A-frames,

Agility has plenty of fun obstacles — from jumps to tunnels to turns to hoops — that are sure to keep your Miniature enthused.

elevated boards called dog walks and others. Basically, the dog must negotiate the obstacles in proper order and style and do it within a set time. The team can strive for high honors, the titles only or simply the joy of working together.

Most training facilities require that dogs have some basic obedience before entering an agility class because your dog must be responsive to you and reliable about not interfering with other dogs and handlers or running off. It is also important to allow your puppy to mature before undertaking agility's jumps and sharp turns because young bones and joints are injured more easily than mature ones.

Again, multiple organizations sponsor agility titles at all levels, from novice through advanced. The rules, procedures and obstacles vary somewhat among the organizations, so it's important to obtain and read the appropriate rule book before entering your dog in competition. In addition to the AKC and UKC, the United States Dog Agility Association and the North American Dog Agility Council also offer agility trials and titles.

The AKC offers Novice Agility, Open Agility, Agility Excellent and Master Agility Excellent titles. To achieve an MX title, a dog must first earn the AX title, then earn qualifying scores in the agility excellent class at 10 licensed or member agility trials.

The USDAA offers eight agility titles. An Agility Dog has achieved three clear rounds (no faults) under two different judges in the starters or novice category of competition. An Advanced Agility Dog has achieved three clear rounds under two different judges in the advanced class. The Masters Agility Dog has demonstrated versatility by achieving three clear rounds under two different judges in the masters standard agility class.

In addition, a dog must receive a qualifying score at the masters level in each of the following: Gamblers Competition, to demonstrate proficiency in distance control and handling; Pairs or Team Relay, to demonstrate cooperative team effort and good sportsmanship; Jumping Class, to demonstrate jumping ability and fluid working habit; and Snooker Competition, to further demonstrate a dog and handler's versatility in strategic planning. To earn a Jumpers Master, Gamblers Master, Snooker Master or Relay Master title, a dog must achieve five clear rounds in the appropriate class. A USDAA Agility Dog Champion has earned the MAD, SM, GM, JM and RM titles. The USDAA also recognizes the Agility Top Ten annually.

USDAA promotes competition by hosting major tournament events, including its Grand Prix of Dog Agility championships. The Dog Agility Masters Team Pentathlon Championship promotes agility as a team sport, and the Dog Agility Steeplechase championship focuses on speed in performance. Dogs must be registered with

These are intense little dogs. After observing different breeds, I've rarely seen such an intense dog once they get on the scent trail of wildlife such as fox, rabbits or squirrels. At home I have to go into the yard and get mine off the trail in order to get them inside. — Miniature Schnauzer owner Scott Andersen, D.V.M., Gambrils, Md.

the USDAA in order to compete in this organization's events.

The USDAA also offers programs for older dogs and younger handlers. The Veterans Program is for dogs 7 years of age or older. The Junior Handler Program is for handlers up to 18 years of age and is designed to encourage young people to participate in dog agility as a fun, recreational family sport.

The North American Dog Agility Council offers certificates of achievement for the regular, jumpers and gamblers classes. The purpose of the regular agility class is to demonstrate the handler and dog's ability to perform all of the agility obstacles safely and at a moderate rate of speed. At the open level, the goal is to test the handler and dog's ability to perform the obstacles more quickly and with more directional and distance control and obstacle discrimination.

At the elite level, more complex handler strategies are tested, with the dog moving at a brisk pace. The dog may be entered in the standard, veterans or junior handlers division. In all divisions, certification in the regular agility classes will require three qualifying rounds under at least two different judges. NADAC also awards the Agility Trial Champion title.

TRACKING

The sport of tracking, as outlined by the AKC, calls for your dog to locate and steadily follow a specific human scent trail that has the distance, age, number of turns and "lost" articles required for that competition level. Titles can be earned based on the type of land covered, either rural, natural terrain or citified surfaces such as pavement and gravel.

Though urban tracking promises to become more popular, most takes place over rural ground. Dogs must work through various types of vegetation, weather conditions, insects, other animal scents and chance encounters with various critters. Since the handler follows at the end of the lead, this tends to be a sport for outdoor lovers.

The breed's usual keenness for hunting and affinity for food blend well in training, as most people initially place treats in their footsteps to keep the dog's head down and create a pleasant association with scenting. Treats are gradually faded until the dog can complete a track without such incentives, instead receiving praise from the handler.

Despite the hardships that go along with tracking, this sport ranks as a frequent favorite among trainers. Most love the early morning outings, time spent exploring the outdoors and watching their dog master an inherent ability far superior to our own.

Many books and videos give step-by-step instructions for teaching your dog tracking, making it one of the easier sports to do on your own. However, nothing substitutes for experienced instruction. Contact your nearest training club to see if any members track, or check the AKC's website for listings of clubs that hold tracking tests.

OBEDIENCE TRIALS

Obedience trials in the United States trace back to the early 1930s, when organized obedience training was developed to demonstrate how well dogs and their owners could work together. Helen Whitehouse Walker, a Standard Poodle fancier, pioneered obedience trials after she modeled a series of exercises after the Associated Sheep, Police and Army Dog Society of Great Britain. Since Walker initiated the first trials, competitive obedience has grown by leaps and bounds, and today

Competitive obedience is a fun way to sharpen your dog's training skills.

more than 2,000 trials are held in the United States every year, with more than 100,000 dogs competing. Any registered AKC or UKC dog can enter an obedience trial for the club in which they are registered, regardless of conformational disqualifications or spaying/neutering.

Obedience trials are divided into three levels of progressive difficulty. At the first level, Novice, the dogs compete for the title of Companion Dog; at the intermediate level, Open, dogs compete for a Companion Dog Excellent title; and at the Advanced level, dogs compete for a Utility Dog title. Classes are subdivided into "A" (for beginners) and "B" (for more experienced handlers). A perfect score at any level is 200, and a dog must score 170 or better to earn a "leg," three of which are needed to earn the title. To earn points, the dog must score more than 50 percent of the available points in each exercise; the possible points range from 20 to 40.

Once a dog has earned the Utility Dog title, he can compete with other proven obedience dogs for the coveted title of Utility Dog Excellent, which requires that the dog win "legs" in 10 shows. In 1977, the title Obedience Trial Champion was established by the AKC. Utility Dogs who earn legs in Open B and Utility B earn points toward their Obedience Trial Champion title. To become an OTCh., a dog needs to earn 100 points, which requires three first place wins in Open B and Utility B under three different judges.

The Grand Prix of obedience trials, the AKC National Obedience Invitational, gives qualifying Utility Dogs the chance to win the newest and highest title: National Obedience Champion. Only the top 25 ranked obedience dogs, plus any dog ranked in the top three in his breed, are allowed to compete.

EARTHDOG

AKC earthdog enthusiast Karen Brittan of Britmor Schnauzers in Oak Grove, Minn., says this sport's perfect for the smallish Mini inclined to go after squirrels, rabbits, mice and other critters due to a high chase instinct and prey drive. "Most dogs absolutely love it once they understand what the game is," she says. "Our Miniature Schnauzer would rather hunt than anything!"

For competition, the dog goes underground through a 9-inch square wooden liner, 30 feet long, until he reaches the caged quarry, usually rats, at the end. He must work the quarry by barking, digging or biting at the bars separating him from the cage. Along the way, the dog will encounter three right-angle turns, and, in upper levels, false scents and narrowed passages.

Training entails getting your dog comfortable entering and moving through a narrow tunnel, turning in total darkness and convincing a breed that normally hunts in silence to vocalize upon finding his quarry. Since the individual aspects of the hunt have specific time limits, speed also takes priority.

"Unfortunately, earthdog events are not as common as some other dog activities, and

SMART TIP!

If you find your schnauzer isn't suited for group activities, once you get your veterinarian's OK and basic obedience training behind you, you and your Mini can find plenty of opportunities for exercise, training and strengthening the bond between you right in your own backyard.

people sometimes have to travel to get to tests," Brittan says. The AKC website lists earthdog-affiliated clubs by state. Local training clubs or terrier clubs may recommend someone willing to help a newcomer.

RALLY BEHIND RALLY

Rally is a sport that combines competition obedience with elements of agility, but is less demanding than either one of these activities. Rally was designed keeping the average dog owner in mind and is easier than many other sporting activities.

At a rally event, dogs and handlers are asked to move through 10 to 20 different stations, depending on the level of competition. The stations are marked by numbered signs, which tell the handler the exercise to be performed. The exercises vary from making different types of turns to changing pace.

Dogs can earn rally titles as they get better at the sport and move through the different levels. The titles to strive for are Rally Novice, Rally Advanced, Rally Excellent and Rally Advanced Excellent.

To get your Miniature Schnauzer puppy prepared to enter a rally competition, focus on teaching him basic obedience, for starters. Your dog must know the five basic obedience cues — sit, down, stay, come and heel — and perform them well. Next, you can enroll your dog in a rally class. Although he must be at least 6 months of age to compete in rally, you can start training long before his 6-month birthday.

If you aren't into sports, make sure your Mini has other activities to keep him busy.

SMART TIP!

Teaching your Miniature Schnauzer to watch your every move begins when you first bring her home. Puppies will automatically follow you, even without a leash, because they want to be with you, especially if you have a treat in your hand. Keep your dog on your left side and offer her a small piece of food with each step you take. In no time, your Miniature Schnauzer pup will think that you're an automatic treat dispenser, and she will never leave your side.

FUN WITH FLYBALL

After seeing her first flyball race, "I knew this would have to be one of the sports I do with my dogs," says Kay DeVeyrac of Calgary, Canada, owner of Kaydees Kennels. "What impressed me most was the fact that these owners were obviously having such a great time with their dogs, and it seemed the dogs couldn't get enough running over the jumps, grabbing their tennis balls and coming back again."

This relay race consists of four hurdles set at a height appropriate for the shortest of the four-dog team. Beyond these hurdles sits a box with a pump-type release that ejects a tennis ball when the dog jumps against it. The goal is for each dog to leap the hurdles, hit the release, catch the ball and return over the hurdles so the next dog can start. Two teams race concurrently, with the fastest time winning.

DeVeyrac, whose dog, Cookie, is a top competitor in the North American Flyball Association, the sport's ruling organization, says the breed possesses all the traits necessary for a good flyball dog. "They're quick learners, want to please and love to run, jump and catch a ball," she says. "They also become intent on the job at hand."

When asked what she personally enjoys the most about flyball, DeVeyrac replied, "It has to be the camaraderie; the human friendships developed over the years and the opportunity for the dogs to socialize. I thoroughly enjoy team sports, and am blessed to have some of the nicest people in the sport on the same team as me and my Minis."

Not as widespread as some other canine sports, flyball lessons can be difficult to find. Check with local training clubs, or contact NAFA for information on teams in your area that could get you started. If all else fails, consider buying your own equipment, finding a few other interested people and establishing your own flyball team.

SHOW DOGS

When you purchase your Mini puppy, you must make it clear to the breeder whether you want one just as a lovable companion and pet, or if you hope to purchase a Miniature Schnauzer with show prospects. No reputable breeder will sell you a puppy and tell you that he will definitely be show quality because so much can change during the early months of a puppy's development. If you do plan to show, what you hopefully will have acquired is a puppy with show potential.

To the novice, exhibiting a Miniature Schnauzer in the ring may look easy, but it takes a lot of hard work and devotion to win at a show such as the annual Westminster

Kennel Club Dog Show in New York City, not to mention a fair amount of luck, too!

The first concept that the canine novice learns when watching a dog show is that each dog first competes against members of his own breed. Once the judge has selected the best dog in each breed (Best of Breed) the chosen dog will compete with other dogs in his group. Finally, the dogs chosen first in each group will compete for the Best In Show title.

The second concept you must understand is that the dogs are not actually compared against one another. The judge compares each dog against the breed standard, the written description of the ideal dog approved by the AKC. While some early breed standards were indeed based on specific dogs who were famous or popular, many dedicated enthusiasts say that a perfect specimen as described in the standard has never walked into a show ring, has never been bred and, to the woe of dog breeders around the globe, does not exist. Breeders attempt to get as close to this ideal as possible with every litter, but theoretically the "perfect" dog is so elusive that it is impossible. (Even if the perfect dog were born, breeders and judges probably would never agree that he was perfect!)

If you are interested in exploring the world of conformation, your best bet is to join your local breed club or the national (or parent) club, the American Miniature Schnauzer Club. These clubs often host regional and national specialties, shows only for Miniature Schnauzers, which can include conformation as well as obedience and field trials. Even if you have no intention of competing with your Miniature Schnauzer, a specialty is like a festival for lovers of the breed who congregate to share their favorite topic: Miniature Schnauzers! Clubs also send out newsletters, and some organize training days and seminars providing owners the opportunity to learn more about their chosen breed. To locate the breed club closest to you, contact the AKC, which furnishes the rules and regulations for all of these events, plus general dog registration and other basic requirements of dog ownership.

MUSICAL FREESTYLE

A stunning combination of obedience, tricks and dance, freestyle is the perfect venue for those possessing an artistic flair. Set within a large, open ring, each handler and dog pair perform a personally choreographed routine in rhythm to their choice of music. A typical presentation might find a dog weaving between the handler's legs as he or she is walking, spinning in place, doing leg kicks and other imaginative moves. Creative handler costumes and fancy dog collars often complete the picture.

Most participants agree that dogs display preferences in music, responding happily to tunes they like while ignoring those they don't. If you're worried about your own questionable dance skills, keep in mind that the self-choreography allows you to focus on your team's special talents.

Find the ham in your Miniature Schnauzer at a local training facility or private trainer. Alternatively, contact the sport's host organizations, the Canine Freestyle Federation and the World Canine Freestyle Organization for information about getting your start in this exciting activity. See Resources chapter on page 166 for more information.

CANINE GOOD CITIZEN

If obedience work sounds too regimented but you'd still like your Miniature Schnauzer to have a title, prepare him for the Canine Good Citizen test. This program is sponsored by the AKC, with tests administered by local dog clubs, private trainers and 4-H clubs.

To earn a CGC title, your Mini must be well-groomed and demonstrate the manners that all good dogs should exhibit. The CGC test requires a dog to follow the sit, lie down, stay and come cues; react appropriately to other dogs and distractions; allow a stranger to approach him; sit politely for petting; walk nicely on a loose leash; move through a crowd without going wild; calm down after play or praise; and sit still for an examination by the judge. Rules are posted on the AKC's website.

NOTABLE & QUOTABLE

Miniature Schnauzers are very quick and smart, and they like having a job. They like being in the thick of the action, and being a team member. They really like the one-on-one time, and they like to have fun.

— *freestyle competitor Morene Stickrod of New Carlisle, Ohio*

THERAPY

Visiting nursing homes, hospices and hospitals with your dog can be a tremendously satisfying experience. Many times, a dog can reach an individual who has otherwise withdrawn from the world. The people-oriented Miniature Schnauzer can be a delightful therapy dog. Although a gentle disposition is definitely a plus, the often normally rambunctious dog seems to instinctively become gentler when introduced to those who are weak or ailing. Some basic obedience is, of course, a necessity for the therapy dog and a repertoire of tricks is a definite bonus. The sight of a clownish Miniature Schnauzer "hamming it up" can help brighten most anyone's day.

Most facilities require a dog to have certification from a therapy dog organization. Therapy Dog International and the Delta Society are two such organizations. Generally speaking, if your dog can pass a Canine Good Citizen test, earning certification will not be difficult. Certified therapy dog workers frequently get together a group and regularly make visitations in their area.

Smart owners can find out more information about this popular and fascinating breed by contacting the following organizations. They will be glad to help you dig deeper into the world of Miniature Schnauzers, and you won't even have to beg!

American Kennel Club: The AKC website offers information and links to conformation, tracking, rally, obedience and agility programs, member clubs and all things dog. www.akc.org

American Miniature Schnauzer Club: The AMSC is the national breed club for Miniature Schnauzers in association with the American Kennel Club. http://amsc.us

Canadian Kennel Club: Our northern neighbor's oldest kennel club is similar to the AKC in the states. www.ckc.ca

Canine Performance Events: Sports help keep dogs active. www.k9cpe.com

Delta Society: This organization offers animal assistance. www.deltasociety.org

Dog Scouts of America: Take your dog to camp. www.dogscouts.com

Love on a Leash: Your sweet Miniature Schnauzer has a lot of love to give others. www.loveonaleash.org

it's a **Fact**

The **American Kennel Club** was established in 1884. It is America's oldest kennel club. The **United Kennel Club** is the second oldest in the United States and began registering dogs in 1898.

National Association of Professional Pet Sitters: When you will be away for a while, hire someone to watch and entertain your dog. www.petssitters.org

North American Dog Agility Council: This site provides links to clubs, obedience trainers and agility trainers in the United States and Canada. www.nadac.com

Therapy Dogs Inc.: Get your Miniature Schnauzer involved in therapy work. www.therapydogs.com

Therapy Dogs International: Find more therapy dog info here: www.tdi-dog.org

United Kennel Club: The UKC offers several of the events offered by the AKC, including agility, conformation and obedience. In addition, the UKC offers competitions in hunting and dog sport (companion and protective events). www.ukcdogs.com

United States Dog Agility Association: The USDAA has info on training, clubs and events in the United States, Canada, Mexico, and overseas. www.usdaa.com

World Canine Freestyle Organization: Dancing with your dog is fun! www.worldcaninefreestyle.org

Don't let your schnauzer sit around all day. Get involved in a dog sport.

BOARDING

So you want to take a family vacation — and you want to include all members of the family. You usually make arrangements for accommodations ahead of time anyway, but this is imperative when traveling with a dog. You do not want to make an overnight stop at the only place around for miles only to discover that your chosen hotel doesn't allow dogs. Also, you don't want to reserve a room for your family without confirming that you are traveling with a Miniature Schnauzer because if it is against the hotel's policy, you may not have a place to stay.

Alternatively, if you are traveling and choose not to bring your schnauzer, you will have to make arrangements for him. Some options are to leave him with a family member or a neighbor, have a trusted friend stop by often or stay at your house. Another option is leaving your Miniature Schnauzer at a reputable boarding kennel.

If you choose to board him at a kennel, visit in advance to see the facilities and check how clean they are, and where the dogs are kept. Talk to some of the employees and see how they treat the dogs. Do they spend time with the dogs either during play or exercise? Also, find out the kennel's policy on vaccinations and what they require. This is for all of the dogs' safety because when dogs are kept together, there is a greater risk of diseases being passed between them.

If your vacation destination isn't Fido-friendly, line up a good boarding place.

HOME STAFFING

For the schnauzer parent who works all day, a pet sitter or dog walker may be the perfect solution for the lonely pet pooch longing for a midday stroll. Dog owners can approach local high schools or community centers if they don't have a neighbor who is interested in a part-time commitment.

When you interview potential dog walkers, consider their experience with dogs, as well as your schnauzer's rapport with the candidate. (Miniature Schnauzers can be excellent judges of character.) You should always thoroughly check all references before entrusting your schnauzer — and opening your home — to a new dog walker.

For an owner's long-term absence, such as a business trip or vacation, many Miniature Schnauzer owners welcome the services of a pet sitter. It's usually less stressful on the dog to stay home with a pet sitter than to be boarded in a kennel. Pet sitters also may be more affordable than a week's stay at a full-service doggie day care.

Pet sitters must be even more reliable than dog walkers because the dog is depending on his surrogate owner for all of his needs over an extended period. Owners are advised to hire a certified pet sitter through the National Association of Professional Pet Sitters. NAPPS provides online and toll-free pet sitter locator services. The

nonprofit organization only certifies serious-minded, professional individuals who are knowledgeable in canine behavior, nutrition, health and safety. Whether or not you take your Miniature Schnauzer with you, always keep your Miniature Schnauzer's best interest at heart when planning a trip.

SCHOOL'S IN SESSION

Puppy kindergarten, which is usually open to dogs between 3 to 6 months of age, allows puppies to learn and socialize with other dogs and people in a structured setting. Classes helps to socialize your Miniature Schnauzer so that he will enjoy going places with you and be a well-behaved member in public gatherings. They prepare him for adult obedience classes and for a lifetime of social experiences he will have with your friends and his furry friends. The problem with most puppy kindergarten classes is that they only occur one night a week.

If you're home during the day, you may be able to find places to take your puppy so he can socialize. Just be careful about dog parks and other places that are open to any dog. An experience with a dog bully can undo all the good your training classes have done.

If you work, your puppy may be home alone all day, a tough situation for a Miniature Schnauzer. Chances are he can't hold himself that long, so your potty training will be undermined — unless you're teaching him to use an indoor potty. Also, by the time you come home, he'll be bursting with energy, and you may think that he's hyperactive and uncontrollable.

The only suitable answer for the working professional with a Miniature Schnauzer is doggie day care. Most large cities have some sort of day care, whether it's a boarding kennel that keeps your dog in a run or a full-service day care that offers training, play time and even spa facilities. They range from a person who keeps a few dogs at his or her home to a state-of-the-art facility built just for dogs. Many of the more sophisticated doggie day cares offer webcams so you can see what your dog is up to throughout the day. Things to look for:

- escape-proof facilities, such as gates in doorways that lead outside
- inoculation requirements for new dogs
- midday meals for young dogs
- obedience training (if offered), using reward-based methods
- safe and comfortable nap areas
- screening of dogs for aggression
- small groups of similar sizes and ages
- toys and playground equipment, such as tunnels and chutes
- trained staff, with an adequate number to supervise the dogs (no more than 10 to 15 dogs per person)
- a webcam

SMART TIP!

Remember to keep your dog's leash slack when interacting with other dogs. It is not unusual for a dog to pick out one or two canine neighbors to dislike. If you know there's bad blood, step off to the side and find a barrier, such as a parked car, between the dogs. If there are no barriers to be had, move to the side of the walkway, cue your Miniature Schnauzer to sit, stay and watch you until her nemesis passes; then continue your walk.

CAR TRAVEL

You should accustom your schnauzer to riding in a car at an early age. You may or may not take him in the car often, but at the very least he will need to go to the vet once in a while, and you do not want these trips to be traumatic for the dog or troublesome for you. The safest way for a dog to ride in the car is in his crate. If he uses a crate in the house, you can use the same crate for travel.

Another option is a specially made safety harness for dogs, which straps your Miniature Schnauzer in the car much like a seat belt would. Do not let the dog roam loose in the vehicle; this is very dangerous! If you should make an abrupt stop, your dog

can be thrown and injured. If your dog starts climbing on you while you are driving, you will not be able to concentrate on the road. It is an unsafe situation for everyone — human and canine.

For long trips, stop often to let your schnauzer relieve himself. Take along whatever you need to clean up after him, including some paper towel should he have an accident in the car or suffer from motion sickness.

IDENTIFICATION

Your Miniature Schnauzer is your valued companion and friend. That is why you always keep a close eye on him, and you have made sure that he cannot escape from the yard or wriggle out of his collar and run away from you. However, accidents can happen and there may come a time when your Miniature Schnauzer unexpectedly gets separated from you. If this should occur, the first thing on your mind will be finding him. Proper identification, including an ID tag, a tattoo and possibly a microchip, will increase the chances of his being returned to you safely and quickly.

An ID tag on a collar or harness is the primary means of identifying a lost pet (and ID licenses are required in many cities). Although inexpensive and easy to read, collars and ID tags can come off or be taken off.

A microchip doesn't get lost. The microchip is embedded underneath the dog's skin and contains a unique ID number that is read by scanners. It comes in handy for identifying lost or stolen pets. However, to be effective, the microchip must be registered in a national database. Smart owners will register their dog and regularly check that their contact information is kept up-to-date.

However, one thing to keep in mind is that not every shelter or veterinary clinic has a scanner, nor do most folks who might pick up and try to return a lost pet. Your best best? Get both!

Did You Know?

Some communities have created regular dog runs and separate spaces for small dogs. These small-dog runs are ideal for introducing puppies to the dog park experience. The runs are smaller, the participants are smaller and their owners are often more vigilant because they are used to watching out for their fragile companions.

INDEX

MINIATURE SCHNAUZER, a Smart Owner's Guide™

part of the Kennel Club Books® Interactive Series™

JOIN OUR ONLINE Club Schnauzer™

LIBRARY OF CONGRESS CATALOGING-IN-PUBLICATION DATA

Miniature schnauzer / from the editors of Dog fancy magazine.
  p. cm. — (Smart owner's guide)
Includes bibliographical references and index.
ISBN 978-1-59378-774-5
1. Miniature schnauzer. I. Dog fancy (San Juan Capistrano, Calif.)
SF429.M58M55 2010
636.755—dc22

2009046640